ROOTS of LABOUR

by

Harry Moncrieff

First published in 1990.
Reprinted 1992
by
Linden Hall, Yeovil BA10 2BW
and
The Industrial Pioneer, Coventry OY3 5EY

Published by:

LindenHall

223 Preston Road
Yeovil
BA20 2EW

and

57 Ulverscroft Road
Coventry
CV3 5EY

ISBN 0 905903 21 7

Cover design and drawings by the author.

Printed and bound by Castle Cary Press, Somerset.

To my father and mother.

Alderman Walter Moncrieff J.P.
and Eleanor Moncrieff (née Townshend)

in proud and loving memory

H.M.

Foreword

by Lord Callaghan of Cardiff, KG, PC.
Prime Minister 1976-1979.

Harry Moncrieff writes with sincerity and affection about a group of pioneers who helped to found the Labour Party – some who were legends in their lifetime, and others who were hardly known even then, but all of whom by their efforts brought into being a party with a mission to end poverty, root out injustice and create a more equal society.

The end of the 19th century saw a great outpouring of enthusiasm, faith and energy that inspired ordinary men and women to deeds that up until then had seemed beyond their power. They removed the taint of the workhouse from children; they understood through their organisation of the 1889 Dock Strike, that they could win their own battles against a heartless exploitation, they aroused an unrepresentative Parliament to the iniquities and indecency of unemployment. It is impossible to read about their efforts without being deeply moved and feeling proud that men and women with little education and no social or economic advantages could achieve so much for their fellows.

To my generation the people Harry Moncrieff writes

about are but names. To young people of today they are not even that. The only one of whom I have any picture in my mind's eye is Ben Tillett. At the end of his life he frequented a Trades Union Club that existed in Newport Street, near Trafalgar Square. I saw him there on several occasions, once most notably when he and the world famous economist J.M. Keynes were ensconced on a sofa and engaged in a salty conversation that embraced us all. The Trades Union Club disappeared alas shortly after the end of World War II.

Harry Moncrieff's upbringing and background has enabled him to convey something of the humanity, the indignation and the sense of injustice that moved the pioneers of the Labour Movement. He reminds us where we came from and what we are here for. After ten years of Thatcherism, our Party has many battles to win if Britain is to become a more just, humane, moral and equal society, and in these days when history, unfortunately, is less well regarded than it was, I hope his book will be widely read and serve as a spur to the efforts of the present day generation.

James Callaghan

Contents

Acknowledgments

I am grateful to Messrs. Cassell, the publishers and Messrs. Macmillan Publishing Co. Inc., the present copyright holders, for the use of material from the following titles:

William Stewart *J. Keir Hardie* Cassell 1921.
George Haw *From Workhouse to Westminster* Cassell 1911.
Robert Blatchford *My Eighty Years* Cassell 1931.

I am also grateful for material from the following:

Ben Tillett *Memories and Reflections* John Long 1931.
Robert Blatchford *Merrie England* Blatchford 1894.
Robert Blatchford *Not Guilty* Blatchford 1906.

I am also grateful for the invaluable assistance of the staff of the following:

The Regents Park College Library (Baptist Union Archives).
Christian Economic and Social Research Foundation
    (Records of the Independent Order of Good Templars).
The Labour Party Library.
The Cooperative Party Library.
The London Borough of Tower Hamlets Library.
The Museum of Labour History.

Also for permission to use the following photographs or make drawings of them:

National Museum of Labour History: Cover and pages 13, 69, 88, 113, 114, 198, 213.
The London Borough of Tower Hamlets: Page 210.

H.M.

Uproot

Between 1740 and 1820 a series of Enclosure Acts brought changes to the long established pattern of life in rural England. Hundreds of thousands of acres of common land were compulsorily acquired and enclosed by private landowners. In the process the rights of many thousands of farm workers to a strip of land for growing crops, and the rights of grazing were extinguished in return for a mere pittance. The landowners on these large fenced fields could now use modern farming methods and make larger profits. Some landowners shared this prosperity with their tenants and workers. Many did not.

It was an agricultural revolution; change was inevitable, but as in other changes at other times the impact on the ordinary man and his family was given little consideration by the landowner, still less by the Government of the day. Better crops no doubt, but how would the new ways affect the people? For some it meant loss of independence, for others, unemployment. Those who had to leave the land to find work lost a whole way of life, the relationship of the family to the community and the common task of growing crops and rearing sheep and cattle.

Traditionally much of industry, outside the mining areas and the ports, was locally based in homes and small workshops serving local needs. Now began the mushroom-like growth of mills and factories, the Industrial Revolution to meet primarily the needs of the export industry. 'Britain the workshop of the world.' The factory offered an alien and unhealthy environment where men, women and children were cruelly exploited and work lost all meaning and dignity. These workers had no voice, no vote, no power.

The Vote

Before the 1884 Reform Act only two and a half million men had the vote out of a population of twenty-five million. The 1884 Act with the 1885 Act brought the number up to four and a half million, adding the agricultural and other rural workers to the still limited franchise of the towns and cities.

Many attempts had been made by working people to make their needs and hopes known over the centuries. Each effort had faded away because there was no effective outlet except small meetings often held in secret and the march or demonstration often brutally suppressed. Working men could now play a legitimate part in the affairs of the land; limited it would be, but it was a turning point. They could now begin to play a part in meeting the needs of the hungry, the overcrowded, the men, women and children suffering appalling conditions in mine and factory and in striving to bring an answer to the waste of lives and talents through unemployment.

Dreams of a new order of mankind took on substance, an order based on the Brotherhood of Man where no man, woman, or child would be alone, uncared for or unfulfilled any more.

I remember an incident when my old grandfather came to stay with us when I was a small boy. I see him standing close to my mother, an old man but still square shouldered and erect; my mother small, hair piled up almost black beside his silver grey, those sharp dark eyes, They had been talking in an animated fashion and then they laughed and burst into song together. It was an old marching chorus:

The land, the land,
'Twas God who made the land,
The land, the land,
'Twas God who made us free,
How can we be beggars
With the ballot in our hand,
God made the land for the people.

Try it to the tune of 'Marching through Georgia'!

'With the ballot in our hand', that was the turning point when between 1884 and 1906 the working man began to make his voice heard in Parliament, Borough and City Councils.

Democracy

What experience of democracy did the working people of Britain have before 1884? In terms of Parliament and Local Government, very little, but in terms of democratic institutions created and run mainly by working people, a great deal. The Craft Unions, the Cooperative Movement, the Temperance Movement and some of the Free Churches were all one man one vote democracies with women playing an equal part.

There was not only a common philosophy and faith running through all of these institutions, but also the experience of how to put peoples' ideas and wishes into shape. Producing policy statements, resolutions and amendments, taking a vote and so producing a basis for collective action, involving all the members in decision making. Few upper class people had this experience, few knew how to run a meeting, how to reach a collective decision. The people who knew how to make democracy work were working people. It was because of this knowledge and experience that in this country they chose democracy and not violent revolution as the basis for their politics.

Dictatorship you impose. Democracy you build.

Man does not live by bread alone, he is capable of powerful emotions. Two are fundamental: self-interest can lead him through fear and hate to exploit his fellow men; while concern for his fellow men can lead him to sacrifice his own needs to meet the greater needs of others.

1833 Compassion

In this year the British Government abolished slavery throughout the British Empire. Millions of Africans had been transported to slavery in British ships — floating concentration camps. It was a very profitable trade. It was also one of the worst examples of exploitation in all history. One man William Wilberforce who was driven by compassion led the campaign for abolition against fierce and relentless opposition. It took forty years of his life. It was part of his campaign to reform the whole moral attitudes of the nation.

1834 Exploitation

In this period English farm workers were the subject of exploitation. Many had been deprived of their small pieces of land and their grazing rights on common land. Then wages were reduced, in Dorsetshire, to seven shillings a week. Six farm workers, Christian men dedicated to non-violence, got together to try to secure some improvement in their appalling conditions. They were taken from families and friends, labelled as 'dangerous revolutionaries' and ordered to be transported to an Australian penal colony for seven years. Later, their innocence, their faith and dignity were recognised and they are remembered as the Tolpuddle Martyrs.

Compassion and exploitation express two opposite characteristics within the nature of man. Within the nature of all men and so of all nations.

Exploitation is not the prerogative of governments. An employer can exploit his workers. Workers can exploit their employer. Husband and wife can exploit each other. It is the root of industrial, social and marital breakdown and war.

Exploitation is demanding without giving.
Compassion is giving without demanding.

Exploitation creates division and conflict.
Compassion can build a new world.

This book is mainly about four of the men who understood and cared about the deprivation suffered by millions of men, women and children in their day. They

each took a distinctive part in building a workers'
movement that in one generation from 1880 to 1910
changed the balance of society.

Poor in Poplar

One day in the year 1855 a ship's engine was started up without the 'all-clear' being given. All was not clear. A stoker named Crooks was greasing the engine. In a horrific accident he lost an arm. He was then out of work with no compensation or income of any kind. Apart from a rare occasional job as a watchman, he never worked again.

Crooks lived with his wife and seven children in one room in Poplar by the docks. His wife was now the breadwinner. Breadwinner is an appropriate term as one of her sons, Will, described later:

> We used to get bread and treacle for breakfast, bread and treacle for dinner and bread and treacle for tea, washed down with a cup of cold water. Sometimes there was a little variation in the form of dripping. At other times there was no treacle or dripping.

Seebohm Rowntree's report on the people of the city of York, under the title 'Poverty: A Study of Town Life' in 1901, spelled out what life was like for the 28 percent of the people of York who lived on or below the poverty line:

> They must never spend a penny on a railway fare or omnibus.

They must never purchase a halfpenny newspaper, or spend a penny to buy a ticket for a popular concert. They must write no letters to absent children, for they cannot afford the postage. They must never contribute anything to their church or chapel, or give any help to a neighbour which costs them money. They cannot save nor join sickness clubs or Trade Union, because they cannot pay the necessary subscriptions. The children must have no pocket money for dolls, marbles or sweets. The father must smoke no tobacco, and must drink no beer. The mother must never buy any pretty clothes for herself or for her children, the character of the family wardrobe as for the family diet, being governed by the regulation 'nothing must be bought but that which is absolutely necessary'.

So it was in Poplar, where many families lived, as the Crooks' family did, in one room with no cooking facilities and with a communal privy and water tap in the back yard.

My mother's family with nine children were a little better off, but not much. Last year I asked her sister Mary, then one hundred years old, where they all slept 'Three in a bed?', 'No', she replied, 'FOUR, yes, two at the top, two at the bottom.' This was how Will slept.

Will's mother worked at home sewing garments for a firm in Houndsditch. Sometimes she sewed all night. One such night Will woke up in the bed that he shared by the wall, he saw his mother sewing with tears running down her face.

As you get older much is forgotten but some incidents, the pictures and the words, remain still sharp and clear. This was one of those incidents for Will, perhaps the first that shaped his life. He recounted it to his friend George Haw:

What are you crying for, mother?
Never mind, Will, my boy. You go to sleep.

But you must be crying about something, mother.
It's through wondering where the next meal is coming from,
my boy.

Will had begun his education for life as he tried to solve
the riddle of why his mother could not get bread when
there was plenty in the shops. And he vowed:

Wait till I am a man, won't I work for my mother when I am
a man!

Will Crooks kept his vow and devoted his life to all the
mothers and the men and the children of Poplar and
beyond.

Workhouse

When Will was eight years old, his mother's struggle to keep them all, so gallantly fought for so long, reached defeat. There was no money, no bread and nowhere for them but the workhouse. The authorities took Will, one of his brothers, and his father. Mrs. Crooks and the rest of the family were sent back on the street to fend for themselves. For a time Will was with his brother, then they were split up, Will being sent to the Poor Law school. Years later Will said, 'Every day I spent in that school is burnt into my soul.' He was haunted by the dread that he must have committed some crime to be taken away from his family and shut up in that fearsome prison-like place.

His mother worked harder than ever, she found a cheap room next door to the casual ward of the workhouse and was eventually allowed to have her children back. Day by day Will saw people like bundles of rags huddled up on the pavement waiting for the workhouse doors to open. He was now back at school and doing a milk round starting at 5 am for sixpence a week.

Will's mother could not read or write herself, but she worked and starved that her children should get some education. She took them to Church and Sunday School. Will owed it to her that he grew up with a love for another poor man, Jesus of Nazareth; a love of books; a decision never to drink alcohol. He was gathering an understanding and strength for a life's work.

Work

At eleven years old he was working in a blacksmith's shop; normal hours six am to eight pm. He discovered *Dickens* and *Scott* and *The Pilgrim's Progress* and the *Iliad*; he used to put on a performance for his workmates with dramatic renderings from *Hamlet*.

My father left school and started work at ten years old, and like Will, he devoured books like a hungry man. He was eloquent in private conversation and could command large audiences in the open air. He was once described as speaking like an educated gentleman. He *was* an educated gentleman. Years later he and Will, twenty-six years senior to him, became close friends.

Will's mother wanted him to have a better chance in life than he would get as a general labourer and so she took him away from the blacksmith's shop and apprenticed him as a cooper. This meant for some years less money but he would be a craftsman, he would have a trade.

At nineteen years old Will Crooks married and saw better times, but not for long. When anything was wrong Will spoke up, whether it was shoddy materials or exploited men. He was sacked and every shop and yard in London was shut against him.

Unemployed in 1876

Will heard that there was work in Liverpool so he set out to walk there.

It was a nightmare journey of days without food, total exhaustion, and at times despair. When Will and many men in those days read Bunyan's *The Pilgrim's Progress* it did not read like fiction. His boots disintegrated, the soles completely gone, a tramp showed him how to use parts of the uppers as soles tied around his feet with string.

Unemployed in 1900

My father was a tailor's cutter and as such he wore the clothes of his trade, top hat and morning coat. He told me once that a shop assistant was expected to dress like a duke on the wages of a dustman. When he was out of work, like Will, he had a problem with his boots. He had worn the soles right through. He carefully cut pads of newspaper that he fitted inside each boot. He had discovered the cheap renewable sole, but it never caught on.

Unemployed in 1932

The dole queue stretched along the pavement and round the corner. It was raining steadily and I was soaked. As I shuffled forward the water squelched in my shoes.

I had been doing so well. I had been working for an architect in North London and I won the gold medal for design at the Regent Street Polytechnic. I remember my cold wet feet, I remember too that the clerk did not look up when he pushed my eighteen shillings across the counter. Back in my little room wedged between my bed and my big drawing board I stuffed newspaper into the shoes to keep their shape and dried them with loving care.

So over the generations we looked after those boots and shoes. We needed them. Unfortunately society did not need us.

Will's walk to Liverpool and back was over 400 miles. My father walked as far. I climbed up, at a rough estimate, the 10,000 stairs of some 200 staircases (architects were usually on the upper floors, solicitors and accountants on the lower).

But there is nothing like a good walk for sorting out

your philosophy. Perhaps the good Lord had to send us on the road to learn. If that was the plan – it worked.

A Poor Man

With his wife's full backing Will kept his childhood vow and remained a poor man serving poor men all his life. He came home one day concerned about a family that were without food. His wife produced a loaf of bread and a jug of cocoa for him to take to them. Years later Will remembered her words. 'All we have in the house, Will, but we've had our own breakfast and they haven't.'

I have sometimes missed a meal but I have never known real hunger. How men, unemployed and hungry, could put their minds to building a new world is beyond all imagining. But they did.

Eventually Will found an employer who appreciated his standards of honesty and workmanship. He worked there for ten years. In those years he began his life's work to bring into the open the plight and the potential of the poor.

Crooks's College

The Rt. Hon. J.R. Clynes wrote of Will Crooks, 'No man of his time did more to awaken the conscience of the nation upon social conditions.'

Will began a series of meetings on Sunday mornings outside the East India Dock gates. This became known among Poplar workers as Crooks's College. He set out to convince his fellow working men that the Local Council and Parliament were there to meet the needs of the people. It was the responsibility of ordinary workers like them to explore what needed to be done and put forward workable proposals, and sooner or later it would be done. He was out to create confident responsible men and women who could make democracy work. Men and women who had clearly earned the right to vote, a right some achieved in 1884. At the same time he made it clear that legislation would not create better men and women. 'That', said Will, 'must depend on ourselves.'

He saw the potential in every man, woman, and child, a divine spark in every one. He would devote his life to blowing that spark into flame, He would teach people to use and develop the institutions of the state as they themselves changed and walked tall.

In his own words at one of the East India Dock meetings:

> Labour may be the new force by which God is going to help forward the regeneration of the world.

Dock Strike

Early on in the years of Crooks's College their work was put to the test. 100,000 London dockers went on strike and brought the greatest port in the world to a standstill. This was the first large scale mobilisation of industrial muscle against exploitation. The quality of the organisation and discipline won an historic victory. Equally important, the discipline of the men earned the understanding and respect of all sections of the community as never before. Will Crooks addressed meetings until late every night and was back before dawn helping with the organisation and the relief stations. During the day he took part in the marches through the City and the West End.

His wife was ill but urged him to keep at it and 'pull those dockers through, never let it be said that your wife kept you from helping those in need.'

No one worked harder than Will Crooks during that epic battle, but his biggest contribution was the thousands of men who had learnt at Crooks's College that their behaviour, their sense of discipline and responsibility could lead the country into a new era.

Ben Tillett was the overall leader with the planning and strategy, John Burns led many meetings and marches, Will Crooks played a major part in producing the disciplined troops. It was not just a reaction against exploitation, it was the beginning of the reorganisation of a great industry.

Testing Time

Will paid a heavy price for his efforts. After it was over he was desperately ill and fighting for his life for thirteen weeks in hospital. Before he was fully recovered he was elected to the London County Council. Within a month of taking office he found himself a widower with six young children, the youngest a baby. For the first time in his adult life he was without the wife's support that had meant so much. Letters of sympathy poured in, not only from his countless friends in Poplar but from political opponents and people from all walks of life. For a year his fourteen year old daughter looked after the home and the young ones, his aged mother gave what help she could, but he knew that he could not go on in that way. Lodging with his mother was a young nurse, Elizabeth Lake, Will asked her to marry him. This remarkable young woman accepted and took on his family, his commitments and Will. They were married in 1893.

Commitment

From Crooks's College had developed the Poplar Labour League. It's first executive consisted of local representatives of the London Trades Council, the Engine Drivers and Firemens Union, the Philanthropic Coopers Society, the East London Plumbers Union, the Federated Trade and Labour Unions and the Gasworkers' Union. The Rev. H.A. Kennedy of All Hallows Blackwall was the treasurer.

Will was offered £500 to go into industry as a manager, a fabulous wage at that time. It was a measure of his ability. The Labour League offered him £3 per week, to include his expenses incurred in his LCC and public positions, if he would work full time for the people.

He quietly closed the door for ever on any possibility of comfort and leisure. In truth his decision had been made as a small boy in that bed by the wall shared with his three brothers. He would be a poor man serving poor men.

Other trade unions later joined the Poplar Labour League and men and women from all walks of life subscribed from time to time, such as Sidney Webb, Bernard Shaw, Canon Barnett and many others.

London County Council

Will now joined the small group of Labour men on the LCC that included:

John Burns	Engineers Union.
Bill Steadman	TUC and MP for Stepney.
H.R. Taylor	Bricklayers Society and one time Mayor of Camberwell.
Ben Cooper	Cigar Makers Union and London Trades Council.
C.W. Bowerman	London Society of Compositors. MP for Deptford.
George Dew	Carpenters and Joiners Society.
W. Sanders	Fabian Society and ILP.

Will Crooks's first speech at County Hall was on a proposal to insert a Fair Wages Clause in all LCC contracts. He called on the Council to adopt Trade Union rates of pay 'in the name of humanity and Christianity.' They were discussing a living wage. The LCC chairman, Lord Rosebery, adjourned the meeting and asked Will to meet him to try to hammer out a compromise. In the event Will's knowledge of the facts of life for the working men and what they needed for a basic existence convinced Lord Rosebery that there should not be a compromise and that the original Labour proposal should stand. The meeting was reconvened and the proposal drafted by Will was moved by John Burns and carried. A small minority of determined men, expert in democratic procedures and armed with a full knowledge of the facts won the day. This episode was typical of the way these men went to work. They brought understanding and, with understanding, support often from unexpected quarters.

As things got done they were widely reported in local and national newspapers and, of course, were eagerly seized upon by labour and trade union papers. In the short period from the 1889 Dock Strike to the General Election of 1906 the whole scene changed for the working man. Poverty and exploitation were still the order of the day, but there was a move from desperate rearguard action to breakthrough. Working men and women had heroes to cheer and victories to celebrate.

Comfortable middle class Tories had to reassess their whole conception of working class people. They had enough problems with their consciences being pricked by men on their own side like Wilberforce and Shaftesbury. Now they had to face members of the working class standing up to them on the County Council. The behaviour of many Tories was as Marx predicted, they dug in to fight the class war. Others like Lord Rosebery learnt to respect a man like Will Crooks; they enjoyed his oratory, respected his arguments, laughed at his cockney stories. These working men opened up their horizons and, it is no exaggeration to say, enriched their lives.

Sir John McDougall, a retired merchant and a fellow member of the LCC wrote years later:

> Mr. Crooks has been my colleague on the London County Council for the last twelve years, and during the whole of that time he has worked with great zeal and ability for the good of London.... His zeal is great, and his wisdom is as great as his zeal. I doubt whether anyone in London has done as much as he in all the measures that tend to the uplifting and the good of the people.

Lord Welby, another LCC member, paid a similar tribute:

Mr. Crooks knowledge, his experience, his courage, his readiness of humour, his good temper and above all, his devotion to the work he has undertaken, have made him one of the most popular members of the London County Council.

He was for a time Chairman of the Public Control Committee, that dealt with weights and measures. He rooted out sloppiness and corruption. The ordinary people knew when things were wrong, and what the ordinary people knew, Will Crooks knew. Coal sacks were commonly undersize and did not hold the full weight, loaves of bread were underweight, standards of quality were being flouted. Many a shopkeeper and costermonger, who had been defrauding poor people, had cause to wonder how Will Crooks had got his reputation as a genial fellow! Honest tradesmen thanked God for him.

On the Parks Committee he was able to get a number of his proposals for parks and recreation grounds in the poorer districts carried through; those included the Bromley Recreation Ground, the Tunnel Gardens of Poplar and the Island Gardens on the Isle of Dogs.

The Municipal Journal published a special number devoted to the Blackwall Tunnel, it reported:

No Councillor·has been so frequent a visitor to the various works, and it is doubtful whether any outsider went so many times into the compressed air.... His popular lecture on the Blackwall Tunnel has been given in all parts of London, to all kinds of audiences, and everywhere the clear, picturesque description Mr. Crooks has given, aided by the lantern and his own genial wit, has made intelligible to Londoners, old, young, rich and poor, what is after all a somewhat dry and difficult subject.

In 1894 in the course of a debate in the London County Council, Will Crooks told of his experience as a boy in a Poor Law School. The Municipal Journal reported:

> Those who heard Mr. Crooks's speech in the Council Chamber, when the subject of the training of Poor Law children came up, will not readily forget it. One of the daily papers, in its admiration the next day, declared it to be the best speech heard in the Council. The speech coming spontaneously with the pent-up indignation of a soul that had suffered sorely from a pernicious system, was a marvellous one, producing a marvellous effect. Councillors in the front benches turned round and visitors in the gallery stretched forward to catch a glimpse of the figure on the Labour bench pleading so powerfully for the children of the poor.

Board of Guardians

Overlapping his work on the London County Council were Will Crooks's other public commitments. In 1901 he was Mayor of Poplar, in 1903 he was elected to Parliament, but his first public office and the key to all the others was his election to the Poplar Board of Guardians in 1890. Working men were now for the first time able to vote and hold office as the result of the property qualifications being reduced and then later abolished. George Lansbury was elected at the same time.

In 1834 a gentleman called George Nichols had been appointed as one of the three Poor Law Commissioners to supervise the operation of the Poor Law Acts as amended that year. He wrote:

> I wish to see the poorhouse regarded with dread by our labouring classes and the reproach for being an inmate of it extended downwards from father to son. Let the poor see and feel that their parish, although it will not allow them to perish through absolute want, is yet the hardest taskmaster, the

closest paymaster and the most harsh and unkind friend they can apply to.

Will took his seat in the same board room where, thirty years before, he had appeared with his mother. He found the officers of the Board administering the workhouse in the spirit of George Nichols, and the Board members indifferent and largely ignorant of what was going on. The members had accepted the position that a Guardian had no right to enter the workhouse except with the permission of the Master, some of the members had never visited the workhouse at all.

They were soon to learn that with Crooks and Lansbury in their midst nothing would ever be the same again. When evidence of malpractices came to their notice action was speedily taken.

A woman inmate escaped and came to see Will. The alarming story she told him about the conditions under which a fellow inmate had died in her arms that night had Will hurrying round to the Institution. He suspended some officers on the spot and they were later dismissed by the Board. To the local Board of Inquiry of 1906 Will stated in evidence:

We found the condition of things in the House revolting. The place was dirty. The stores were empty. One day I went into the dining room and found women sitting on long forms, some sullen, some crying. In front of each was a basin of what was alleged to be broth. They called it greasy water, and that is exactly what it looked and tasted like.

The staple diet when I joined the Board was skilly. I have seen old people, when the stuff was put before them, picking out black specks from the oatmeal. These were caused by rats, that had the undisturbed run of the oatmeal bin.... Sometimes there were quarrels about food. I have had to protect old and weak men against stronger men who would steal what was eatable from their dinners.

There were always two sides of the coin as far as Will was concerned. On a later occasion the women were creating a fearful uproar, he writes:

> I went to the Dining Hall. There was dead silence the moment I entered. 'I am right down ashamed of you. When you were treated like animals, no wonder you behaved like animals. Now that Mr. Lansbury and I have got you treated like human beings, we expect you to behave like human beings.'

Later in the day the ringleader came to apologise. There were no more scenes like that.

Within five years of his election Will was made Chairman of the Board and held the position for ten years. In those years efficient and humane administration was established and the Poplar Union was the model among Poor Law Authorities and frequently commended by the Local Government Board. Gradually the old workhouse and school officials who had run the institutions as they liked were weeded out. Food, clothing and sick nursing were improved out of all recognition.

There was opposition to the Crooks/Lansbury revolution and a Municipal Alliance was formed, they put out stories that reached the Local Government Board. The President came down to see for himself, he issued a circular recommending all that Poplar had introduced.

Will Crooks's aim was to get the children out of the workhouse. At a Guildhall Poor Law Conference he said:

> Surely it is far cheaper to be generous in training Poor Law children to take their place in life as useful citizens than it is to give the children niggardly training and a branded career.

So he got the children into the ordinary schools, into separate residential homes, into decent clothes, so that they were made to feel like ordinary working class children. He spoke of the stream of starving people who knocked on his door:

> Do you think that I can finish my own breakfast after being called to the door to listen to these pleadings morning after morning? Do you think, after these daily experiences, that I care how the outside public and the Press attack us because we as Guardians dare to spend public money in saving these people from starvation? What is the Board of Governors to do, with its awful responsibilities and awful obligations, during such distressful winters as Poplar sometimes witnesses? Remember, we live among the poor. We are not carriage folk who can return to the West End and talk about the poor over dinners of a dozen courses. What else can we do but try to keep the bodies and souls of these poor people together in times of trade depression and cold weather?

The Guardians' school at Forest Gate was four miles from the Union buildings in Poplar. Even with five or six hundred children always under training at the school there were batches of neglected children left in the workhouse. Will's scheme was to get them into decent clothes and into surrounding schools. The London School Board objected most strongly but as usual Will had prepared his case meticulously and won the day. He helped to banish all that suggested pauperism from the Forest Gate School. These children were educated and grew up, not branded as workhouse children, as before, but like the children of working parents.

HM Inspector of Schools reported:

> There is very little (if any) of the institution mark among the children... both boys and girls schools are in a highly

satisfactory state, showing increased efficiency, with increased intelligence on the part of the children.... They compare very favourably with the best elementary schools.

Will pleaded and won the right that the Poor Law Schools should receive scholarship and technical education grants as other schools. One of the great moments of his life was when he opened a letter from the headmaster at the Hunslet Poor Law School. 'In consequence of what you have done, one of our boys has just taken a County Scholarship. The first Poor Law child to do so.'

Lord Salisbury appointed Henry Chaplin to his Cabinet of 1885, as President of the Local Government Board. Soon after taking office he sent for Will Crooks and the two spent a morning discussing the weak points in the Poor Law system. Mr. Chaplin made many notes and on parting said Will Crooks had given him enough work to occupy the next two or three years.

Mr. Chaplin declared emphatically for the Poplar policy, and issued circulars to Poor Law Guardians, that gave the support of the Government to the humane administration of the Poor Law that Crooks had established at Poplar. It laid down three principles that Crooks had urged upon the President at their first meeting:-

1. Children to be entirely removed from association with the workhouse and the workhouse surroundings.

2. Old people of good character who have relatives and friends outside not to be forced into the workhouse but to be given adequate out-relief.

3. Old people in the workhouse of good behaviour to be

provided with additional comforts.

The Asylum Board

Mr. Chaplin also invited Will to be one of the Local Government Board representatives on the Metropolitan Asylum Board. He was twice reappointed to this position by Mr. Chaplin's successor. The Asylum Board had, at that time, fourteen infectious diseases hospitals with accommodation for nearly seven thousand people, four asylums accommodating six thousand people whose condition merited, in those days, the title of imbeciles.

It was also responsible for several boys on a Thames training ship and two thousand children in various homes. The members of the Metropolitan Asylum Board were a very select company and they were somewhat astonished when in May 1898 a working man from Poplar arrived in their midst, the nominee of a Conservative Cabinet Minister.

For the first five months he never spoke at the Board meetings. He explained that he was 'learning the business.' Later he was to become Chairman of two committees, the Children's Committee, and a special committee to reorganise the hours and wages of the Board's large staff. He had learnt the business.

'How is it, Mr. Crooks, that whatever you ask this Board for, you always get?', he was once asked by a former Chairman. His joking reply was because he was always right, but his real secret was that he did his homework and he set out to convince every single member of the Committee. If he had not convinced them all, rather than push his view through with a narrow majority he would often say, 'Let's take it home with us, perhaps after a week's thought you'll come back convinced to my view. If not, then you must come better prepared to convince me that I am wrong, than you are now.'

Few men had higher ideals or felt more deeply the injustice of the existing social system, but Will recognised that the only way to get reform was to make the best use you can of the present machine and not wait for the millennium.

A Parliamentary Committee recommended that children with physical or mental trouble should be transferred from the London Guardians to the Asylum Board. There were two thousand of them. Another job for Will. It took a substantial part of his time over the next three years.

New homes were set up in the country and at the seaside for afflicted and convalescent children. They were given good food and non-institutional clothes. They got out in the fresh air and played games. To Will their laughter was better medicine than the doctor's, for him as well as them.

Children brought before a magistrate for a first offence were often remanded in prison. Will argued:

> These children want keeping as far as possible from both prison and the workhouse. We ought to put them in small homes and give them school time and play time like other children, until their cases come before the magistrate again.

This was done and several houses were taken and adapted as Remand Homes.

The Bow Street magistrates were sympathetic but had to say it was unlawful. 'We'll alter the law then', said Will. He saw the Home Secretary and put it to him that the Juvenile Offenders Bill that was actually before Parliament could be amended to keep these children out of prison or the workhouse. The amended Bill was passed into law the following month.

Assets

Typical stories of these children:
  A sad eyed little girl in a blue frock:-

> Me and my sister was taken up by the police for sleeping on a doorstep.
> Why on a doorstep?
> Father left us and when mother died the landlord turned us out.

A small boy:-

> Me and my brother we found a donkey and 'barrer' at Covent Garden we saw a man's name on the 'barrer' and 'fought' if you went off 'wif' the donkey we would get a shilling the next day for taking it back to him. But a 'copper' stopped us as we was leading the donkey over Waterloo Bridge. So we hadn't a chance to take it back as we was going to.

Will was on the side of boys and girls like this, he believed in giving them plenty of work and plenty of play. Direct their energies wisely and they would grow up to be useful members of society. He said, 'If there is any part of the community that can be called a national debt, it is this class of poor, misguided lads who, if they were properly cared for, would soon be a valuable national asset.' I cannot imagine that anyone before had ever called these children 'assets.'

The attitude of Will Crooks was completely revolutionary in those days, and he was fiercely attacked by some people in high places as were people like Wilberforce and Shaftesbury. Will Crooks did not see slum children as a social problem, but boys and girls that he knew by name in the streets of Poplar. He loved them. Love is to see the potential in a person that those who do not love do not see. Love is not blind, only hate is blind.

It would seem that everyone for miles around ran to Will's little house at 28 Northumberland Street, to the north of East India Dock Road, when there was trouble.

A small girl came to the door one night with the announcement: 'If you please, father's took to drink again, and mother says will Mr. Crooks come round and give him a good hiding.'

An old labourer who could neither read nor write arrived on his doorstep: 'Well, Charlie, what's the matter now?', 'She's turned me out again, if you would only go and speak to her, Mr. Crooks.' A month later Charlie hails Will from across the road, 'Mr. Crooks I don't know what you said to my ole woman that night, but she's been a perfect angel since!'

'Mr. Crooks, my husband Dick took a drop too much at the 'Ship' last night, and when he came in, me having gone to bed, he mistook the paraffin oil bottle for his medicine. Two whole spoonfuls he took, Mr. Crooks, and we've only found out this morning he says he must see you now afore he dies.'

Will had personal friends in the Peers' House as well as in the Poor House, but his manner never changed in the company of either. Nor did his cockney stories.

His work brought many to his door: C.B. Fry, the cricketer, G.K. Chesterton, George Bernard Shaw, Beerbohm Tree, Earl Carringham and visitors from abroad.

Proud of the Poor

One day after he had shown a party of titled people at their request round some of the dark corners of Poplar, someone suggested tea. 'It's no use looking for swell tea shops in Poplar', said Will, 'But if you care to come with me, my wife will just be getting tea ready for the children coming home from school.' So they arrived at his house without warning and sat down to tea with the children at the deal table in the kitchen.

He took a learned professor to see how the poor lived one cold winter's morning. One woman told him: 'Hunger we can sometimes stand, 'cos we gets use to it, but to be frozen with cold on top of the hunger – that's the thing that makes you squirm, guv'nor – ain't it, Mr. Crooks.' Nearby on the muddy ground a woman sat cursing. 'Ain't been living here long, Mr. Crooks', volunteered another woman, 'her husband's no work, and this morning she was a-sending her four children to school without a bite, so I calls 'em in here, and shared out what we was having for breakfast.' 'And what was that', asked the professor. 'It weren't ham and eggs', she replied. 'Tell my friend what you gave them, Mrs. B', said Will. 'Well, my man's out of work himself, and we only had one loaf, so I cut it up between her children and mine.'

As the two men came away Will said:

> I'm proud of the poor, and it's a dirty insult for outsiders to say these people are degraded by the feeble efforts I make as a Guardian to give bread to the hungry. It's nothing to what they do for each other. That woman sharing her last loaf with another woman's children is typical of what you'll find in every street and corner of Poplar where the pinch of hunger is felt... sometimes people as badly off as these come to my

house in the morning, begging me as a Guardian to give their children bread before they send them to school. Do you think, after these daily experiences, that I care how the outside public and the Press attack us because we as Guardians dare to spend public money in saving these people from starvation? Remember we Guardians live among the poor....

Mayor

In November 1901, even though the Labour Party was only half a dozen strong on the Council, Will was elected Mayor of Poplar. He had agreed to stand only on condition that he should not be paid. He was the first working class Mayor in this country.

One of the first meetings he attended as Mayor was a meeting of London Mayors called by the Lord Mayor at Mansion House to consider arrangements for Coronation Dinners for the poor. When he rose to speak he was shouted down and the Lord Mayor had to intervene. 'Gentlemen', he said, 'I protest against this conduct. I call upon my friend, Mr. Crooks, to speak.' They had forgotten that Will and the Lord Mayor (Sir Joseph Dimsdale) were colleagues on the County Council. Sir Thomas Lipton, who represented the King at that and subsequent meetings to organise the King's Dinner for the poor of London, declared afterwards that the one man who seemed to know what was wanted was the working man Mayor of Poplar. The Mayors who had shouted him down elected him to the small subcommittee that carried out the final arrangements. Will's arrangements for feeding twenty-five thousand people in Poplar went off without a hitch. It is as well that the King had chosen to visit Poplar as the arrangements in some West End boroughs were a disaster. In the event the King was unwell and the Prince and Princess of Wales visited

Poplar on his behalf and chatted happily with the Mayor and Mayoress.

The Lord Mayor invited Will to a City banquet. He wore his blue serge suit, all the other guests were in court-dress, uniform or evening dress. When Will walked through the reception room after being announced the crowded company broke into rounds of applause. At the coronation ceremony in the Abbey, Will asked to be exempt from wearing Court dress, the King gave him the exemption he asked for.

Will had arrived and was accepted in all quarters and on his own terms.

Since the Labour Mayor was debarred by what he called 'his chronic lack of wealth' he was unable to entertain at his own expense. His election was celebrated at a dinner by the Poplar Labour League on 11 January 1902. Lord Monkswell sat at the table with stevedores and gas workers. Nearly every trade and every church in Poplar was represented. Dean Lawless of the Roman Catholics, the Rev. Nairn of the Presbyterians, Father Dolling of the Anglicans, sat down together for the first time in their lives!

Dolling wrote:

> I think it was just splendid. It is given to few men to gain the respect, confidence, and esteem – I might say affection – of friends and foes, colleagues and opponents. God grant you strength and perseverance.

The Roman Catholic Dean wrote:

> God bless you and God speed you, and also your gentle wife, the Mayoress.

Elizabeth Crooks took her position as Mayoress in her stride and was the same calm outgoing person whether attending a conference of working women or receiving the Prince and Princess of Wales.

Will brought about many changes in the Borough's administration, introducing something of the business like methods of the LCC. He was able to further some of his plans for the Borough including obtaining a gift to build three additional public libraries. A presentation was made to him and Mrs. Crooks by all parties on the Council at the end of his year of office. 'Had we known what a good Mayor you would be', said one of the Conservative members, 'we should never have opposed your election.'

Old Age Pensions

Will set out to make life in the workhouse less like life in prison. He also wanted to keep worn-out old men and women, who had friends and family prepared to look after them, out of the workhouse. This meant making the much discussed old age pension a reality. He made a statement to a meeting of the National Committee on Old Age Pensions, of that he was a member:

> For two or three generations the working classes of this country have been asked to vote for Doodle or Foodle and Old Age Pensions. The elector of today, like his father and grandfather before him, is still waiting for the fulfilment of that promise, many may die of old age still waiting, perhaps ending their days in the workhouse. Now I for one got tired of waiting. I have commenced to pay pensions already. I maintain that it is both lawful and right to pay pensions through the Poor Law. And I intend to go on paying them, until Liberal and Conservative politicians cease deluding the people by promises and establish a State system.

To the argument that this is only a system of 'glorified out-relief', he argued:

> So are most pensions, out-relief to the poor is no more degrading than out-relief to the rich.... Cabinet Ministers and Civil Servants are paid old age pensions. Look down you may on these veterans of almost endless toil, but don't forget they have fought in the industrial army for British supremacy in the commercial world and won it. The least their country can do is to honour their old age.

We have to remember that Will was Chairman of the Poplar Board of Guardians for ten years. He had interviewed many hundreds of men and women who were old, sick and destitute, who had kept up the struggle to maintain this independence as long as they could. When they pleaded for a small sum in relief and begged not to be sent to the workhouse, he saw his own mother standing there. Will said, 'Why do I say pay pensions through the Poor Law? Because it is here and so long as we have the system I'm going to make the best of it.'

He claimed before the Local Government Board Inquiry into the Poplar Guardians' administration that he was within the law in doing so. He quoted from a circular issued by Mr. Henry Chaplin as President of the Local Government Board and a member of Lord Salisbury's Government:

> The Local Government Board consider that aged and deserving persons should not be urged to enter the workhouse at all unless there is some cause that renders such a course necessary, such as infirmity of mind or body, the absence of house accommodation, or of a suitable person to care for them, or some similar cause; but think they should be relieved by giving adequate outdoor relief.

It would appear that Will Crooks won the day, but in practice there was a long way to go, and fierce and often unscrupulous opposition was waged against him and his colleagues.

Parliament

Admiral Lord Charles Beresford resigned his seat as Member of Parliament for Woolwich on 18 February 1903, on being given command of the Channel squadron.

A Mr. Geoffrey Drage was nominated as the Conservative candidate, and Will Crooks by the Woolwich Labour League Representative Association. Lord Charles Beresford had been elected unopposed in 1900, and in 1895 his majority was 2805.

The Labour Association quickly raised £200 for the campaign, but to reach the 16000 voters on the register and cover all the other costs, a much larger sum was required. A public appeal for funds was sent out by the Association and the Daily News opened a Woolwich Election Fund. Contributions poured in, shillings and sixpences from working men and women. Colleagues on the LCC contributed about £100 between them, the Rt. Hon. Sydney Buxton, Mr. George Cadbury, members of the clergy including Dr. Clifford, the Rev. Stopford Brooke and Canon Scott Holland.

Support came from every progressive section in the constituency, the temperance societies and the churches all gave support. Keir Hardie wrote to the electors describing Will as, 'a first class fighting man, and the best of fellows, who would, if returned, bring credit and honour to the constituency.'

John Burns addressed a meeting of over 5000 people

while the crowds held up the traffic. He described Will as a man who, 'pursued his ideal with brotherly love and Christian charity.'

My father was a street corner speaker in this campaign and my mother a door to door canvasser. They used the lessons learnt in this campaign years later to get my father elected by an overwhelming majority in my home town that had never before had a Labour man on the Council. Will's opponents knew something about 'dirty tricks' as some do today, they spread the rumour that as he was a poor man he would have to be paid a salary of £500 a year out of the rates. Will replied that he had been in public life for fourteen years and never had a halfpenny from the rates in that time, and if he remained in public life another fifty years he would still never have had a penny from the rates.

In his election address he said:

> If I can further the well-being of my country by assisting in the developing of a nation of self-respecting men and women, whose children will be educated physically and mentally fitted to face their responsibilities and duties, I shall be content.

The vote was:

Crooks (Labour)	8687
Drage (Conservative)	5458
Majority	3229

Congratulations poured in to the little house in Poplar from John Burns, Keir Hardie and David Shackleton from the House of Commons, from dockers at Middlesbrough, coopers at Birmingham, Sir Henry Campbell-Bannerman, the Hon. Maud Stanley, Lord

Tweedmouth, Sir Wilfrid Lawson, Mr. Beerbohm Tree and many ministers of religion. From the Bishop's House, Kensington, Dr. Talbot wrote:

> I desire to express great satisfaction that the needs and interests of Labour should have their representative in one who has given such proof of desire to work and suffer for the welfare of his fellow men as you have done. All that I have heard of you commands my admiration and respect. May you seek, and may God Almighty give you, the wisdom and strength to use rightly this great position.

Good wishes came from nearly every public house in Woolwich where he was well known for his talks on all manner of subjects. The support was remarkable because Will was a teetotaller and active in the Temperance Movement. He had made many a meeting roar with laughter over innumerable stories he told during the campaign against beer drinking. Messages came from Europe, America, South Africa, and Australia. Children were always writing to Will, and now they sent their congratulations and good wishes. The election came within weeks of the famous Newcastle conference of the Labour Representation Committee whose delegates represented over one million workmen. The Conference had decided on absolute independence for the Labour Party. Almost the first duty of its secretary, J. Ramsay MacDonald was to issue an appeal, 'to everyone in London interested in the foundation of a Labour Party in the House of Commons to go to Woolwich to help Mr. Crooks.'

The Rt. Hon. J.R. Clynes wrote:

> His success was very largely personal but it was a Labour success and at once stimulated great hopefulness in the

country and a resolve to build the Party firmly and be ready for a General Election.

Will prophesied 'What the workman has done in Woolwich you will find he will do in other towns.' Three years later in 1906, 29 Labour candidates were elected, some with huge majorities. One prominent man declared at the time, 'This is the Party that was born at Woolwich.'

Compassion

It was demonstrated in Woolwich and in many elections since that people wanted a more compassionate government, and Labour politicians such as Will Crooks expected workers to demonstrate that compassion in their day to day lives.

A Labour MP sat in my home in 1950 he said, 'When we won the election in 1945 I thought there would be a wave of enthusiasm through the country, production would soar, there would be a new spirit. But it didn't happen. It didn't happen.' He was a broken man, he had built his life on an unsound foundation. The men of 1903 had not. Democracy, socialism, a compassionate society was not just about power in Westminster, it was also about men who built sound homes and cared for their fellow men.

So in 1903 at countless meetings at dock gates and up and down the country Will Crooks preached responsibility and discipline and helped to create a caring fellowship at street and dock and factory level. People who by the way they lived would undergird the policies. My disconsolate MP friend had forgotten this, if he had ever understood it.

Unemployment and a Living Wage

At Westminster with Keir Hardie and the few Labour members and sometimes with Liberal support, Will Crooks regularly raised the problems of the unemployed and the underpaid. A fortnight after his election to Parliament, he raised the question of the 21 shilling a week wage being paid to workers in the national workshops. On these wages a man could not afford to keep a family on the standard that Local Government was now requiring in a workhouse.

He used to tell the story of how he made a protest to a Government official against the low wages paid to women in the Government's Victualling Yard at Deptford. 'It's starvation', he told him, 'to pay widows with families 14 shillings a week.' 'But it's constant', said the official. 'So you see', says Crooks, 'that Government officials think starvation's all right so long as it's constant.'

He raised the question of election expenses and payment to members so that all sections of the community could be properly represented. All his speeches were closely argued, with facts and figures to support his case, and there was always the Crooks humour. On the question of payment for members he quoted an advertisement he had seen in the *Yorkshire Post*. 'MP, a gentleman, thirty, holding a responsible position in London, desirous of entering parliament wishes to meet with an affectionate and wealthy lady, view matrimony. Genuine. Highest credentials.' Although the proposal was talked out by the Government his speech produced laughter and cheers.

In the election Will had advocated votes for women. He introduced, in the House, the Women's Enfranchisement Bill that had been drafted by the ILP. The second reading was not reached when the session closed, much to the relief of the Government. In his speech Will had said:

> It is because in all my public work I aim at making people self reliant, able to think and act for themselves, that I want women to have the power and the responsibilities that the possession of the vote gives.... We entrust to women as teachers and as mothers the all-important work of educating the future citizens. How absurd, then, to hesitate to give women the rights of a citizen.

In 1904 Will raised the question of feeding necessitous school children and a Bill was introduced in 1905 that would give local authorities permissive powers to feed school children 'unable by means of lack of food to take full advantage of the education provided for them.' The Bill only reached its first reading, but it prepared the way for a successful Bill the following year.

In February 1909 the government reduced income tax by ten million pounds while Crooks was advocating that this money and more should go to establish Old Age Pensions.

Will became one of the most popular speakers in the House. He was always well informed and his style was lively and conversational, full of wit and telling illustrations He cared so deeply about underfed school children, the unemployed, the taxation of food and such like issues that he won the good will of both sides of the House and frequently the votes.

A policeman on duty in the House asked, 'Well, Mr. Crooks, how's Poplar?', 'You know Poplar?', 'Yes, I used to be stationed that way. I well remember your dock gate meetings. I liked the Poplar people better than the West Enders. You take it from me, Mr. Crooks, there's far more respect for law and order in Poplar than there is in the West End.' In fact Will was still continuing the 'Crooks's College' meetings down in the docks in Poplar.

The Labour Party was organising for its great political triumph of 1906. Will Crooks addressed Labour meetings all over the country, nearly always with an audience of three or four thousand. He was at Glasgow, Birmingham, Leicester, Plymouth, Liverpool, Exeter, Darlington, Ipswich, Chatham, Newcastle, Blackburn, Barnard Castle, Huddersfield, Edinburgh, Cardiff all within a few months. In between he addressed church, temperance and many other organisations.

Crooks's three years in Balfour's Parliament had a remarkable triumph in the Unemployment Act. It was generally agreed at the time that this Act would not have seen the light of day and certainly not passed but for his untiring advocacy. Sir William Chance, one of the bitterest opponents of the measure, described it as 'a Poplar Bill framed to meet Poplar's needs.' And so it was. There was 24 percent unemployment in areas of the East End of London at that time. The Bill was based on the principle that had guided Crooks in all his dealings with the unemployed, that was to provide them with useful work in preference to relief. He had applied this in the workhouse, abolishing useless and uneconomic labour such as oakum-picking and introduced work such as clothes-making and bread-baking.

As far back as September 1883 he was appealing in the *Daily Chronicle* to the Board of Trade and the Thames Conservancy to put unemployed men to work reclaiming foreshores. As usual he had done his homework, quoting the powers provided under the Foreshore Act of 1866 and an 1857 Act empowering the Thames Conservancy to reclaim miles of foreshore; he also quoted the success of similar schemes on the banks of the Forth and Tay.

Meanwhile Will got on with the job in Poplar. With the Rector of Poplar a committee was formed backed up by the Bishop of London and Canon Scott Holland, an appeal raised £5000. Gradually Will changed the committee from a relief committee into a committee providing work. He received an offer of £1000 from Mr. A.F. Hills, of the Thames Ironworks, on condition that he should raise a similar sum. The Borough Council promptly voted £1000 and men were put to work repairing roads and lime-whiting courts and alleys. Public bodies were accepting the responsibility to provide work. Will realised that the response of the men employed had to be good or support for such schemes would quickly collapse. If a man was offered work and failed to turn up he was refused relief if he applied for it. Drastic measures, but there were powerful forces ranged about Will and his colleagues.

Will was appalled at the indifference of the British public and the widely held view that the unemployed were a shiftless, good-for-nothing class. He was well aware that hunger and unemployment over a lengthy period demoralised and degraded people, he knew that a man driven into the workhouse often remained there for the rest of his life. It was this callous waste of lives of people who were potentially a national asset that distressed him.

At the opening session of 1904 he seconded Keir Hardie's amendment to the Address regretting that 'in view of the distress arising from lack of employment no proposal was made for helping out-of-work men.' He advocated practical schemes for putting men to work based on the experience gained in Poplar. He also advocated training men in agricultural work that would make them better fitted for work at home or in countries such as Canada. The appeal to the House fell on deaf ears.

Crooks, Hardie, Lansbury, and others were not to be put off; they met with Mr. Long, the president of the Local Government Board. The result was the calling of the Unemployment Conference at the Local Government Board on 14 October 1904. Crooks and Lansbury presented the Poplar proposals; some were immediately accepted by Mr. Long. Others were adopted by the Government. These were the 'Poplar Proposals':

1. The president of the Local Government Board to combine the London Unions for the purpose of dealing with the unemployed and the unemployable.

2. Such central authority to take over the control of all able-bodied inmates in London workhouses.

3. Farm colonies to be established by the central authority for providing work.

4. Local Distress Committees to be also set up, consisting of members of Borough Councils and Boards of Guardians, to work on the lines already laid down by the Mansion House and the Poplar Distress Committees.

5. The cost to these local committees of dealing with the urgent need occasioned by the want of work to be a charge on the whole of London or on the National Exchequer, instead of being a charge on the locality, always provided that the payment given be for work on lines similar to those adopted by the Mansion House and the Poplar Distress Committees.

6. Rural District Councils to be asked to supply the Local

Government Board with information when labourers are wanted on the land, such information to be sent to the Local Distress Committees.

7. Parliament to take in hand the question of afforestation, the reclamation of foreshores, and the building of sea walls along the coast where the tide threatens encroachment.

Almost immediately after the Whitehall Conference Mr. Long formed a Central Unemployment Committee for London, personally arranging that Crooks and Lansbury should become members. He also advised the formation of local Distress Committees by the Poor Law and Municipal Authorities.

The situation was desperate that winter. The *Daily Telegraph* and the *Daily News* between them raised £30,000 for relief in West Ham. The Poplar Guardians did not give money to a starving family if the husband was fit to work, but did give a few shillings worth of food. This was cheaper than putting them in the workhouse. This minimum assistance cost a fourpence increase in the rates and was violently attacked as an extravagance.

The Poplar Guardians pressed for an emergency session of Parliament. They were supported by fifty-six other Poor Law Unions and eighty Municipalities throughout the country. The Prime Minister, A.J. Balfour, did not think anything would be achieved by this means and refused.

At this time Will Crooks's health, undermined by years of overwork eventually broke down and he was very seriously ill. Sympathy and affection poured in from people in all walks of life. He recovered but was never fully fit again. On 18 April an Unemployment Bill was introduced into Parliament and a Royal Commission on the Poor Law appointed. However within a week of the adjournment of the House in August it was still not through all its stages. At the last moment the Government brought the Bill forward. The *Daily News* of 5 August reported on 'the strange story of the passing of the Unemployment Bill' and said:

> At the end of last week its chances seem to have disappeared. Today it has passed Committee, and Monday will see it through the Commons. The Member chiefly responsible for this is Mr. Crooks, who has shown undoubted subtleness as a Parliamentary tactician.

In the opinion of many people well able to judge the distress and discontent in the country the Act came just in time to prevent serious disorders in the large towns. The Distress Committee formed under the Act got to work. However the weakness of the Act was that it provided finance for the expense of organising work, but not to pay the wages of those employed.

The women of Poplar met in the Town Hall with Elizabeth Crooks in the chair. On 6 November 1905 six thousand women marched on Whitehall. The inscription on their banner was 'Work for our men – Bread for our children.' It was cold and wet, some of the women carried their babies and were unable to prevent their skirts dragging through the mud that was deep along the Embankment.

Mrs. Crooks said they had come as English women, driven to despair, in the hope that the Premier, as the chief minister to the King, would no longer leave them in a worse condition than that of his dogs and horses. Mr. Balfour was sympathetic but he saw no hope of Parliament voting any money. They were sent empty away on the long trek back to the East End.

Before a week had passed another woman spoke. On 13 November, Her Majesty Queen Alexandra issued an appeal:

> I appeal to all charitably disposed people in the Empire, both men and women, to assist me in alleviating the suffering of the poor starving unemployed during this winter. For this purpose I head the list with £2000.

Before the winter was over £150,000 had been subscribed.

The Queen had backed the initiative of the men and women of the East End of London and put Parliament to shame.

Will was in great demand as a speaker on such occasions as the annual meeting of the Baptist Union, whose President was his friend the Rev. John Wilson, one of his best supporters in Woolwich. He often spoke at the London Wesleyan Mission, and regularly at the Sunday afternoon meetings at Poplar Town Hall with the Rector of Poplar. He always spoke in the same forthright manner, on one occasion he rose in the House to speak on the Licensing Bill, his first words were, 'I wish to take the opportunity, while the Prime Minister is in the House, to say a few words on the subject of temptation.' He was speaking about men who failed to resist the temptation of drink (we would call them alcoholics today). His concern was not to offer such people condemnation but help.

The Churches

He was invited to address the National Free Church Council at their annual meeting in 1906. The President, the Rev. J. Scott Lidgett, in introducing Will said that the invitation had not been given to him lightly. It was a deliberate recognition of the claim that Labour had upon the thought, energy, and prayers of the Free Churches. Labour and the Free Churches were joined in their endeavour to solve some of the great human problems.

Shortly afterwards he was asked by the Free Church Council to speak at a dinner to celebrate the return of nearly two hundred Free Churchmen to the House of Commons. He said in the course of his speech:

> You Free Churchmen have to come out of yourselves a great deal more in the future than you have in bygone days. You cannot live for Sunday alone. You have to live for all seven days of the week, and we expect you to come out and take a share of the work of social reorganisation. I have been told plenty of times that poor men and women are not God-fearing. Aren't they? I know the stories they tell you parsons sometimes; but down at the bottom of their hearts is a deep religious feeling that some of us would be better for having. Why can I always get the truth from the poor, who so often deceive you parsons? Why, because they feel I am a brother, and they have a doubt about you. You have got to wear that doubt off. You have got to make the humblest of our brothers and sisters understand that you really do care for them, that you intend to use the Parliamentary machine to abolish sweating and slumdom. We have got to provide industry in such a way that every honest worker may find useful work to do. We have to deal with the shirker whether he wears a top hat or hobnail boots.

After many years of hard public service, Crooks saw some of the things for that he had striven so strenuously adopted as part of the policy of Guardians, Council and Government. Woolwich re-elected him at the General Election of 1906 with over nine thousand votes, three hundred and thirty-nine more than it gave him, three years before, at the famous by-election.

Enquiry

In the meantime vested interests and reactionaries led and financed by the Poplar Municipal Alliance continued to snipe at the works of the Poplar Guardians. Eventually their effort succeeded in persuading the Local Government Board to set up an enquiry into the administration of the Poor Laws in the Borough of Poplar. Will Crooks, still the Chairman of the Guardians, welcomed the opportunity to put the evidence of their work before the public. Hundreds of men and women, boys and girls, who had been regarded as a burden on society were stepping out of Poplar institutions to a new life as decent, useful citizens. What had the Guardians to fear? Quite a lot as it transpired.

It was not just the Poplar Guardians under the Chairmanship of Will Crooks who were on trial, but a clash between two basic attitudes to the old, the sick, the starving, the unemployed, all commonly lumped together as 'the poor.'

Some regarded them as unfortunate human beings having the potential to do well given the opportunity.

Others regarded them as an inferior breed beyond redemption.

Will Crooks and the others like him, as practical Christians, took the first view. The Municipal Alliance the second.

The man appointed to conduct the enquiry, James

Davy, was an officer of the Local Government Board. His sympathy was entirely with the Municipal Alliance, he wanted to get the Poor Law administration back to the repressive principles of 1834.

There were no legal rules for such an enquiry although there were well established precedents that could have been followed. James Davy chose to ignore precedent and conducted the enquiry in his own way, the procedure was a travesty of justice.

On the first day of the enquiry a lawyer, Mr. F.E. Robb, instructed by the Municipal Alliance was invited to make an opening speech. He was dealing with the business of housing and feeding hundreds of people, it was a big business. It soon became evident that he was speaking not just for the benefit of the enquiry but also the Press. It was what we would call today a 'propaganda exercise.' Mr. Robb spent a great deal of time reading out masses of figures relating to the amount and cost of provisions bought under a whole series of contracts. These figures would, of course, seem enormous to any ordinary person familiar only with household accounts. The scope for bribery and corruption in the placing of contracts was described, but no proof that any had occurred was offered. The attempts of Crooks and Lansbury to ask questions or comment were refused; Mr. Robb must have his say without interruption. For the first fifteen of the twenty-one days that the enquiry lasted James Davy allowed Mr. Robb and the Municipal Alliance to have control.

Disgruntled officials who had been dismissed were invited to Whitehall to give information in secret, the Chairman and Vice Chairman of the Board of Guardians were not allowed to be present to hear this 'evidence'.

Extravagances in the provision of clothing was alleged, individual items being produced from the mass of accounts such as 'boys linen collars.' Why should workhouse boys have linen collars? No answer was allowed until days later, in the meantime the *Daily Mail*, the *Daily Mirror* and *Punch* had got their story and their headline. The answer was simple; some of the boys were going out to schools and were provided with collars and other clothing so that they would not be different to the other boys. The purchase of items of girls clothing were also raised; these it turned out were for girls who were leaving to go out into the world to jobs that had been found for them. If Crooks had his way none of these children would have been placed in the workhouse in the first place; as it was they were his boys and girls and he fought for them as he would for his own. When people talked in the presence of Will Crooks about workhouse brats they often forgot that this large black-bearded man had once been one of them.

A cartoon appeared depicting Crooks and Lansbury smoking cigars and ordering a fresh barrel of beer from the workhouse cellars. Both these men were teetotallers and non-smokers, it is inconceivable that the editors and staff of national newspapers and journals would not have known this.

Eventually Corrie Evans QC was allowed to appear for the Guardians well into the second week of the Enquiry. He produced witnesses to put some of the story straight and demolished the credibility of some that Mr. Robb had relied on. But the damage was done.

James Davy's report to the Local Government Board was inaccurate and biased; its object was to discredit not so much the men concerned but the whole attitude to the 'paupers' shown by Crooks and Lansbury. He wanted to punish the 'paupers' so that they felt of the Poor Law as George Nichols wanted them to feel back in 1834.

Aftermath

In the Borough Council elections, that followed soon after the enquiry, the smears in the Press cost Labour many seats, except in Poplar where the truth was well known. Here Labour won many more seats and votes than before. George Lansbury defeated the Chairman of the Municipal Alliance and one of its members wrote to the press:

> I did not think, when we embarked on this expensive trip, that we were going to attempt to cover with ridicule men who, it must be admitted... are now proved to have been thoroughly honest in their policy.

Will Crooks replied to the Report on behalf of the Poplar Board of Guardians and took up three issues. Regular out relief payments to old people that it had been said amounted to a pension; corruption; and the problems of a borough such as Poplar with a disproportionately high level of poverty and unemployment:

> The State pensions its well paid Cabinet Ministers and officials; and we claim under the 43rd Act of Elizabeth that the poor (not merely the destitute but the poor) are entitled to come to society in time of need.

> We neither palliate nor excuse any lapses either on the part of members or officers of the Board, but we claim that as a Board we have carried out our duties as efficiently and as economically as we are able, we have never given

indiscriminate relief.... We have tried to do our duty both to the poor, who have our first claim, and to the ratepayers.

We have never ceased to urge for the past ten years that the poor are a metropolitan charge, that unemployment is a national question, and that the Poor Law should be reformed. We are glad to know that our work, despite the present attacks, has been successful, and that the poor of Poplar are better cared for, and that not only the poor of Poplar, but the poor of the United Kingdom generally as a result of our effort.

The Labour Party, backed by Conservative Members, pressed the Prime Minister for the opportunity to discuss the report. Keir Hardie and Will Crooks pointed out that an injustice was done to a popularly elected body, the effect of that would be to deter other Boards of Guardians from carrying out the Poor Law in a humane spirit.

The Prime Minister, pathetically out of tune with the mood of the country, wriggled out of the Government's responsibilities by informing the House that the report was not made by the Local Government Board, but to that Board by one of its officers!

God Bless You Mr. Crooks

After the Enquiry Will, in spite of his failing health, spoke at a series of tremendous meetings across the country. His meetings in Poplar and Woolwich, where he was supported with rousing enthusiasm, were the largest he had had in those boroughs. At Chesterfield where he addressed an open-air meeting of nearly twenty thousand Midland miners, his reference to his Poor Law policy was cheered to the echo. The Cleveland miners were equally enthusiastic when he went up to their annual gathering.

It was the same at public meetings in Newcastle, Bristol, Huddersfield, Rossendale, Stockport, Batley, Sunderland, Penarth – the man who had stood out against Bumbledon's fiercest onslaughts had the goodwill and confidence of the working people of England. At his indoor meetings there were rarely fewer than two thousand people present. Outdoors he had audiences of four and five thousand. After one meeting he wrote:

> How good the people are! Whenever I mention Poplar, it is truly inspiring to hear the magnificent response. Last night the moment the word passed my lips an audience cheered like one man. It sometimes overwhelms me almost. Who am I to deserve it?...

He had letters of apology and support from political opponents and Government officials and encouragement from ministers of all denominations, and many from people not known to him from America, France and other countries. From the pulpit, press and universities the Poplar evidence was being quoted and praised. The message was that what the Poplar Guardians were doing now must, in the long run, become national policy.

Will Crooks spent all his life in Poplar, poverty was never far from his doorstep. He chose not to escape from it but to stay and answer it. He knew the evil that blinkered men and an uncaring system could do; as a small, hungry and bewildered boy he had been banished to the workhouse while his mother was returned to the streets. Had this experience made him a bitter man he might have become a man with a cause; but he would never have become a man with an answer.

Will Crooks's love for men, women and children extended, like that of his Master, to all men, good and bad, rich and poor. People behaved better because of him as he kept his vow to be a poor man serving poor men.

An old man typical of many, came up to him after a meeting and said, 'Let me shake you by the hand Mr. Crooks. We read about it in the papers, but the papers don't understand. We've been through it and we know. Don't be down-hearted, Mr. Crooks, God bless you.'

The Woolwich Tabernacle

The nineteenth century saw working people developing their own culture independent of the upper classes and the State. This was demonstrated in many fields including religion. One example was in the working class area on the south bank of the Thames where the Woolwich Ferry crosses. During the eighteen seventies a little fellowship of Baptists met in a house in Robert Street and later, as their number grew, in Bethlehem Chapel in Charles Street. By 1878 their membership had grown to ninety and the Principal of Pastors' College sent a young Scottish student, John Wilson, to be their student pastor. He stayed on as their pastor until he died in 1939, after over sixty years of service. During those years John Wilson and this fellowship became a great influence on the life of the local community and far beyond. Out of their own resources they built a great church.

Before this great enterprise was started they took over a larger chapel at Parsons Hill and hired the local Drill Hall for their Sunday services. It seated two thousand people. Typical of the people who came were the workers at the Woolwich Arsenal, by far the largest employer in the district. Craftsmen and labourers, foremen and managers, they came not just on Sundays but to a variety of meetings every evening in the week.

The social activity in the Woolwich area produced not only the work at Parsons Hill, it produced the Royal Arsenal Cooperative Society, one of the largest and most efficient cooperatives in the land, and the only one affiliated to the Labour Party. There were several lodges of the great Temperance Movement, the Good Templars; and a local Labour Party that antedated the formation of the Labour Representation Committee nationally. This local body invited Will Crooks to stand for Parliament at the famous 1903 by-election, organised and financed the campaign and won a startling victory.

My mother and father, like many others, took an active part in all these activities; the Parsons Hill Baptists, the Royal Arsenal Cooperative Society, the Good Templars, the local Labour Party. Each of these organisations gave an expression to one aspect of the lives they lived. Each one had a one man (or woman) one vote democratic constitution.

There was no radio or television in those days to give people packaged views and vicarious activity; they formed their own views and put them into practice with people they knew. Thousands of men and women in this one district learnt to make democracy work.

Everyone who was concerned about any aspect of the life of the community knew they had an ally in the Rev. John Wilson whether they had any religious convictions or not. Hundreds of people who met him through some good cause were grateful for his help and encouragement and many through him found a faith.

In the late eighteen eighties the Parsons Hill Baptists were filling the Drill Hall on Sunday evenings and so they began to think of a larger chapel of their own and set up a building fund. In 1891 they appointed a Building Fund

Committee. My mother, then aged sixteen, was among the young people who helped raise the money.

By 1894 they had raised a substantial sum and appointed an architect to draw the plans. I have a copy of the report produced by the Fund Secretary that accompanied the architect's plans, it is written in a large sloping hand and lists the costs, the construction, the materials, the heating and ventilation and the seating – 1520 in the chapel, 1000 in the semi-basement hall, four more rooms seating a further 232. The Woolwich Building Society had some faith too; they lent them part of the money so that an immediate start could be made, (a sum soon repaid!).

The foundation stone laying of the Woolwich Tabernacle was in June 1895. It is recorded that the platform was filled by leading citizens and that a huge assembly surrounded the site. This was not just a Baptist occasion, it was an occasion in which the whole community joined. On 8 July 1896 the Rev. Thomas Spurgeon, Pastor of the Metropolitan Tabernacle preached the first sermon in the completed building. In 1903 my mother and father were married by the Rev. John Wilson in the Woolwich Tabernacle.

Charles Booth surveyed the religious influences in south-east and south-west London, in that same year 1903, he was impressed by the spiritual vitality evident in the Woolwich Tabernacle, he referred to 'this congregation of artisans' – men who provided the deacons, found the money and took a big part in the work. Two hundred young people gave their spare time to teaching and helping among the 1000 children during the two sessions of the Sunday School every Sunday, and two hundred in the Band of Hope. There was preaching and testifying in mission halls, in lodging houses and at street corners. Charles Booth remarked also 'a tendency towards a greater gaiety than was characteristic among Baptists.'

Many organisations in the Borough when they needed larger accommodation for special occasions were welcome to use the chapel itself or the lower hall. This helped many good causes and forged a link between them and the members of the Tabernacle. School children, unemployed, soldiers from the local barracks, crowded into 'magic lantern' lectures and social functions and many leaders in social and political work addressed meetings.

When she was one hundred years old my Aunt Mary told me about those early days when she was a girl in Woolwich. She was vague about recent happenings but if you asked the right question it was like switching on an old film as she described the picture that flashed into her mind. I taped one conversation:

'Aunt Mary, I remember my mother saying that when she was a girl your sister Eliza made herself a red dress to wear when she went with your brothers to see Arsenal play, is that right.' A snort of laughter from Aunt Mary, 'Ha – the red dress – yes – they were happy days a a better than today – people don't know how to enjoy themselves today.' 'But they were hard times, Aunt Mary.' 'Oh yes they were hard, but they were good times.' 'And when your mother died, my mother Ellie, brought you all up.' 'That's right she was eighteen and I was seven – there were nine of us. Ellie was the best of mothers to us – she was strict, made us do everything that we should. She gave us money for sweets, a halfpenny – sometimes she hadn't got a halfpenny and gave us a farthing and said we had to share them!'

'And you went to the Woolwich Tabernacle.' 'Oh yes we all did – the good old Woolwich Tabernacle – it was wonderful

– it was always full – up the top (the gallery) and the bottom, we used to sit in the gangway and on the steps, which we weren't supposed to do – there were crowds outside, they couldn't get in they stood in the street and joined in the singing.' 'And there was a band to accompany the singing?', 'Yes and they used to play in the square too – down by the steps, by the Ferry.'

'And you used to play the piano at home', 'Yes – and Ellie she used to play too. We used to stand round – and sit on the floor – and we'd have a good old sing-song – they were lovely times – sometimes I sit on the end of my bed now and have a sing song all by myself – and the Matron comes and tells me off.' She demonstrated by singing a chorus of 'Pack up your troubles!'

She was sad that people, particularly young people today, don't have such good times as she had. She said, 'They don't realise there's a God.... I know... when I'm ill he comes beside my bed' she said this in a quite belligerent voice. You had better believe it. God had walked with her all her life, a life shared with her own family and in her younger days at the 'Good old Woolwich Tabernacle.' Happiness was synonymous with togetherness. Possessions meant little to her (except the piano!). She left school and went into service at twelve years old. She was poor and had to work hard right up to her mid-nineties but she would not have traded that life she had for all the tea in China.

It is recorded that years later when the Rev. John Wilson celebrated the fiftieth anniversary of his arrival in Woolwich:

With one accord, his own people, his fellow citizens, his brother ministers, and his denominational peers, along with the Bishop of Woolwich and the Roman Catholic priest, united to do him honour.

The relationship between Free Churches, the Church of England and the Roman Catholics at that time varied from unease to antagonism, but not in Woolwich.

Anyone who has attempted to give some service to the community in political, charitable, or religious work will know the painful experience of division between people who should be working side by side. John Wilson brought people of differing backgrounds and beliefs together to an extent that few men have achieved. One thing is certain, he did not do it by compromise. His faith was unwavering, his commitment to his Master total. These qualities did not 'put people off' they drew people to him.

Quintin Hogg invited John Wilson to join him in building up the Woolwich Polytechnic, and like Will Crooks in Poplar, he worked for the poor as a Guardian and on School Boards. He was a member of the Council of the YMCA. He had a passionate desire to see every child with a good job and a good education, thousands got that chance through his work and advocacy.

John Wilson was elected only the second Freeman of the Borough of Woolwich and a new street was named after him. He accepted none of the many honours given to him as personal to him but said, 'I am proud of the services which have been given to Woolwich by members of the Tabernacle.'

A member of the Woolwich Tabernacle wrote after the death of John Wilson:

> The true memorial of any good man's life, it has been said, is his influence carried in the lives of others. From the moment young John Wilson entered Charles Street Chapel in 1878 until his victorious end in the first week of 1939, he spent

himself in the service of the people of Woolwich – in their homes and streets, in their councils and places of business, in their chapels and among the resting places of their dead – an ambassador of Christ and the brother to all. Visible memorials of him exist in stone; his gracious influence will live on earth long after the day he passed over and 'all trumpets sounded on the other side.' The people of Woolwich lined the streets as his body was borne to the grave.

Small Giant

Ben was born in John Street, Bristol, on 11 September 1860, he was the youngest of eight children. His mother died when he was just over one year old. His father could not cope with the household and the children. A stepmother and relatives fared little better. Ben, the youngest, was largely left to his own devices, uncared for and unloved.

One side of John Street backed onto the Easton Coal pit. The hoists and derricks and the rocker arm of the pit pump were black against the sky and coal dust shrouded roofs and walls and pavements. Life in John Street was lived against an angry roar of sound, clangs and crashes from cage and wheels, tubs and trucks, metal against metal, and the whine of a prop-cutting circular saw. A huge roaring fire hole threw out a blaze of heat and cast weird shadows. It needed only a few horned devils and a monster to complete a picture of hell.

Ben was warned not to go near the noisy frightful pit head, but curiosity and hunger drew him. There he learnt to make himself useful filling tea cans with water and putting them on red hot bars to boil.

In return he got scraps of food and mugs of tea, kind words and the occasional clout. He almost belonged. It was an apprenticeship to the world of work. A childhood world of love and play and books and music Ben never knew.

Later he became a regular wage earner in a brick-yard. Bricks were individually hand moulded, a similar process to making bread. Ben's job was to cut a huge lump of clay into the right sized oval balls for the brick moulds, each ball weighing seven or eight pounds (rather heavier than bread!). It was enormously hard work for a lad and required no little skill and judgement. If he cut a ball too big for the mould the surplus chunk would come hurtling back at him from the moulder, striking him on his neck or back as he bent over the bench. Some days in summer they worked from 5 am till dusk.

Ben was below average height and weight. He was six years old.

Brick-making was only a summer job; in the autumn he took to the road with a stray dog as his companion. He learnt from tramps and gypsies how to survive outside the constraints of law and society. Part of his learning was how to fight with his fists and to handle a stout stick as a weapon. There was an unquenchable spirit in Ben. In an age when many waifs and strays did not survive, Ben was a survivor.

Next he joined a circus run by a family friend. He learned acrobatics, cared for animals and played his part in the eternal tasks of pitching and packing up the big top and the side shows. He shared a bed of straw with his dog, Ginger, and a pony.

It was not so much a romantic adventure, more one long back-breaking grind. But to Ben it was worth all that to be part of a marvellous comradeship. Up till now it had seemed like Ben against the world.

Eventually Ben was 'snatched from the sawdust' by one

of his sisters and sent to school for the first time, when he was just past his ninth birthday. The discipline, the injustice, the unimaginative teaching methods revolted him. He was too old in the ways of the world to accept all this without question. One day, with no justification, the teacher rapped Ben's knuckles with his ebony ruler, Ben threw himself at the totally unprepared young man and left him spread-eagled on the floor. Thus started and ended Ben's one and only short period of formal education.

So back to the road, in his own words:

> I was a lawless young ruffian, taking a job where I found one and leaving it when I felt inclined to wander away in search of fresh adventures.

What hope could there be for such a boy? I learnt from my father never to write anyone off. That there is a God-given potential in every man. I have not always found this doctrine easy to accept, still less to apply. But if there was ever an example of its truth it was Ben Tillett.

Over fifty years later the Rt. Hon. Philip Snowden MP wrote of him:

> He has, to a greater extent, I think, than any man I have known, the gift and the power to move vast bodies of men by his eloquence and sincerity. He is a superb master of polished diction. His appeals are never addressed wholly or mainly to men's material interests, but to their manhood and self-respect.... Workers thronged to his meetings in their thousands, and came away having seen the vision of a new Earth.

Yes, this was Ben Tillett, and not one word that Philip Snowden wrote was an exaggeration. He became a maker of history, a giant among men.

To Sea

Ben had before him more years of hard demanding physical effort governed by often ruthless discipline. At the age of thirteen he joined the Royal Navy. He joined as a ship's boy at Plymouth aboard the old *Impregnable*.

He was so small they had no shoes or clothes to fit him. Clad in ridiculous outsize clothes Ben might have been a figure of fun, his spirit crushed. But he learnt his craft with the same enthusiasm, eager to do his best, and he fought anyone, of any size, if he had to.

For every one of the multitude of tasks to be performed aboard there was a technique to be learnt. Instant obedience was enforced with harsh discipline, sometimes with brutality, but every hand aboard knew that if they forgave you the sea would not. Ignorance and slackness on the high seas cost the lives of men and ships. A seaman did not need Darwin to give him a lesson in the survival of the fittest.

Ben was taught to holystone, scrub and swab the decks, to clean iron, steel and brasswork fittings and the big guns. He got to know every one of the sails and the maze of halyards, sheets and clewing gear; and to go aloft furling and unfurling, reefing, lashing and stowing; he learnt to repair sails using palm and needle. He learnt to take the wheel and steer by the compass, to handle a small boat under oars or sail, and to make and mend his own clothes. Later he learnt to use cutlass, rifle and pistol and to take his place in a gun crew.

He was being taught to turn his hand with knowledge and skill to any task needed to take a ship to sea and to bring her home. Even if cold, wet and hungry, when 'Hands aloft!' was called the last man was in for a whipping, blows or kicks, sometimes even the cat-o'-nine-tails.

After the first year Ben's weekly pay was doubled from threepence to sixpence.

Ben loved the sea and ships; the hardship did not bother him; he had rarely, if ever, in his young life slept between clean sheets or sat at a dining table with table-cloth, china, glass and shining cutlery. Ben not only learnt about each part of a ship, he grasped the total entity of hull, spars, rigging, sails and men. He stood in awe of the immensity of the sea and sky, wind and wave, and the fact that a stout ship and a disciplined crew could master the vast power of the elements.

The potential of a disciplined body of men was the lesson that he learnt at sea. It was a lesson he was to apply, a few years later, while still a young man, when he masterminded a great enterprise, that involved one hundred thousand men, the Government of the day and the City of London.

After his early training, Ben joined the Sealark, a small fast and lively brig, he was the royal yardsman and the champion at races over the cross trees. Later he sailed in the Resistance, a battleship of the Channel Fleet, where in another such race, high above the deck, he caught a foot as he made a swinging leap and suffered a severe hernia. He was ever grateful for the surgeon and nurses who dealt with this injury, for what would be a routine piece of surgery today, was a chancy business over one hundred years ago. He was discharged from hospital and the navy after only three years in the service.

He was soon back at sea in a full-rigged merchant ship sailing out of Bristol and bound for America. He was still only sixteen but it would be ridiculous to think of him as a boy. He was a seaman.

This first voyage encountered the normal share of gales and one crew man was lost overboard. In quieter moments the men ran racing competitions with the large maggots out of the biscuits, and Ben learnt to make decorative carvings out of a piece of salt beef that polished like mahogany. When they reached the Delaware the voyage had taken months instead of weeks.

The return voyage was fast, but Ben spent much of it at the back-breaking work of trimming the vast shifting ocean of grain in the hold. While they were still at sea that grain would be bought and sold several times over in the market, the only danger to the huge profits made was that the seamen did not get the ship home at all.

There was a host of ships at sea around the coast of Britain in those days, wooden ships, nearly all dependent on sail alone, fishing boats, barges, colliers, merchant ships often overloaded and sometimes carrying deck cargo. They sailed in all weathers, the crew frozen with cold in the winter, often wet through for days and even weeks on end; there was constant danger and many ships were lost. I have seen a chart marked with the location of the graves of the 3000 ships wrecked around our coasts in the one year 1872.

Who can put a value on the sailor in peace and war? Yet in those days there was no compensation for injury or death. Nothing for the widows and orphans.

Welcome to Docklands

After a voyage to the West Indies, Ben went to see his sister in Bethnal Green. This welcome can be best described in his own words: 'The door was opened by a vigorous able-bodied, middle-aged woman who gave me a hearty welcome and a mother's hug, the first hug of a woman I remember.' Ben had found a rough comradeship in the circus and on the sea both born of a desperate struggle for existence, but in Bethnal Green he found a home and undemanding love. He was like a soldier home from a long war who could at last take off his armour.

There was a-seven-year old called Newton in the house, presumably a relative, and Ben became attached to the lad and took responsibility for him. In teaching Newton to read he developed his own limited reading capacity.

Ben, as a child, had experienced the squalor of the life of a tramp on the road and the appalling hardship of a seaman's life, but now as he walked the streets and docks of East London seeking work, he saw poverty, filth and degradation worse than anything he had ever imagined. There was widespread unemployment and experienced dockers had literally to fight to get work. Ben's chances were slight. Years later he set down his impression of the 'cage', the iron rails that protected the man selecting dockers for work and the men:

> In a building that would hold very few in comfort, men were packed tightly almost to suffocation; this struggling mass fought tigerishly, elbowing each other, punching each other, using their last remnants of strength to get work for an hour or half-hour for a few pence. The strong literally threw themselves over the heads of their fellows to get near the rails of the 'cage' that held them like rats. We poor wretches hung around for 'calls' at any period of the day or night, and were kept for a week at a time hungry and expectant for the work that never came.

For several years Ben alternated between seeking work ashore and off again to sea; sometimes coastal work or the continental ports and trips as far as the Russian port of Riga. The work ranged from the sheer slog of trimming coal in the hold, to the skilled and dangerous work aloft securing splintered spars and shredded sails. But he was determined to settle down ashore in spite of the problem of finding work. He eventually found a job at the Monument Quay warehouse at London Bridge, where he worked for several years, his first steady job except for his three years in the Royal Navy.

Now in his early twenties Ben married and established his home in the back room of a house in Bethnal Green. His work was carrying sacks of tea up and down stairs in a tea warehouse, shifting many tons each day. Late into the night he continued the reading and study he had begun with the lad Newton. He bought books whenever he had a few coppers in his pocket. He was reading Hazlett, Wordsworth, Samuel Johnson, and so on to Huxley, Spencer, Darwin and Thomas Carlyle, even Cardinal Newman and 'Gladstone's dreary contributions to the controversy between religion and science.' He was learning Latin and trying to learn Greek. He appreciated the clear thinking of the agnostic Charles Bradlaugh and Annie Besant; in later life he was to get to know them both, but their philosophy did not capture him because there was what he called a 'strain of mysticism' in his nature, a religious instinct that could not be denied.

Like many of the leaders of those days he was determined that the working man in spite of his harsh treatment by society, should do all he could to improve his own quality of life. This led him, along with Hardie, Lansbury, Snowden, Crooks and many others, to join in the work of the Temperance Movement. My mother and father both held high office in the Temperance Movement and it was there that, around 1900, they met many of these men as well as in the Independent Labour

Party and the Baptist Church.

Ben took part in agitation for better pay and working conditions for the dockers; he was well aware that little or nothing was being achieved, but he was learning to present a case and hold an audience. He knew that it was going to need some vast heave, mass organisation, an impact on the employers, something to stir public opinion. Many street corner agitators (and the breed is not extinct), having passionately  described WHAT was wrong and even more particularly WHO was wrong, left the matter there. Ben was not concerned with mere protest he was concerned to know HOW the situation was to be changed. He did not know.

A Friend

In a mood of despair and pessimism he went to see his friend Cardinal Manning. In later life he described Manning as 'the kindliest and greatest man it has been my good fortune to encounter.' Manning, as one would expect from a wise Christian long in experience, drew out from Ben what was on his heart. This was, of course, to produce a better life for the men and families in dockland. He encouraged Ben to commit himself to the task to which he had been called, and not to concern himself with success or failure. He held out no prospect of an easy road; quite the reverse, he used the phrase, 'you cannot wear a crown without bearing a cross.' This stern doctrine did not deter Ben Tillett, he described this meeting as an inspiration. He was ready.

Now it is normal Christian experience that once the commitment is made, particularly if it is anchored with a friend like Manning, the opportunity opens up. When it came, Ben described it in these words, 'the miracle happened'.

1887 Dockers

One day in July 1887 the management of a warehouse in Cutler Street announced that they would reduce wage rates for the men handling the new season's tea crop.

The men were on starvation wages already so they called a meeting of all the men in the warehouses of the London docks. Ben was asked to represent the men in his warehouse. The invitation was brought to him by a brawny giant of an Irishman called Fleming, who had dropped his real name of Flanagan because many jobs were advertised 'No Irish Need Apply.' Ben went along to the meeting with Fleming and one of his closest friends, a lay preacher, Harry Orbell. Ben described the scene:

> The room was full of hot, excited, sweltering men, the clamour and vociferation was deafening. A man called Prentice took the chair and made a rabid confused statement of the position. Indignation was the dominant note, and I could see the whole agitation petering out in ineffective denunciation of the employers.

The giant Fleming lifted Ben onto the table, gripped him fast with his massive hands, and urged him to speak. Without Fleming the moment would have been lost. With the extra height of the table it was now Ben who was the giant, but – he had a stammer, his tongue was dry, his throat constricted. He had to speak:

> I knew the meeting wanted direction, a clear indication of how to proceed. I knew we wanted machinery, a base, a starting point, a controlling authority. So my stammering lips, tripping me the more rapidly I spoke, urged the necessity of organising, suggested the method, urged the selection of a Committee with the power to frame rules, and to issue an appeal to the organised workmen of the country.

His proposals were supported with enthusiasm. A collection of twopence each was taken from all present. Ben was elected to the Committee of twelve that was appointed and immediately went into session. Ben was appointed Secretary to receive a wage of £2 a week. When the Committee meeting broke up the faithful Fleming was waiting outside for Ben.

And so the Tea Coopers and General Labourers Association was born and Ben Tillett accepted the post of Secretary and held it for thirty-four years until the amalgamation that formed the great Transport Workers Union, in which he also held office. Ben Tillett was the only man who had gone to that meeting in the Oak Tavern with any sort of plan of action. Now he had to justify it.

There was no body of support. General labourers were statistically referred to as 'unskilled', 'the Salvation Army cared for them but did not minister to the self-respect of the casual worker', wrote Ben. These were harsh words. The Salvation Army cared for individuals however poor or wretched they were, and for this they should have been given full credit, but they did not have the vision that Ben Tillett had of transforming the status of a whole class of men. How many people did?

The Craft Unions, in the main, opposed the idea of unions for the 'unskilled.' To them a union preserved the status of a craft for men who had served a seven-year apprenticeship. To associate with the 'unskilled' could only reduce their status, so they would have none of it. I remember a workman saying to me years ago 'Class, class, there's no bigger class distinction than between a plumber and his mate.'

The dock workers, themselves, during the first twelve months were mainly apathetic, some antagonistic, Ben and his colleagues at their outdoor meetings had stones and refuse thrown at them. The biggest task was to give the men faith in themselves. Society had ground them down.

Ben called them 'dockers'; he may have coined the term. He saw the dockers standing with the seamen and the miners as men who could hold their heads up high in any company.

All Ben had was a dozen or so willing helpers, a few pounds, and a piece of paper with some names on it. He had no full-time help. He had moved onto a big stage, after all he had a stage army. But in less than two years it was to become a real army, trained and disciplined.

He started with a mass meeting on a Sunday morning in July 1887 for 2000 or 3000 men by the bandstand in Victoria Park. The word went out, mainly by word of mouth, to the 100,000 workers from the docks, wharves and warehouses of the Port of London.

Ben Tillett also wrote personal letters to Members of Parliament, leading churchmen and other eminent people. In these letters he set out the conditions under which dockers worked and the case against the employers. He asked for advice and support and invited them to the meeting. The clarity and scale of his vision evoked response.

Among others, Sir Charles Russell MP (later the famous judge, Lord Russell of Killowen) wrote, 'I shall gladly help in any practical plan.' Professor James Stewart wrote, 'Combination is the watchword of the working classes.' George Howell MP, Secretary of Trade Union Congress risked the anger of many of the craft unions by offering help. Samuel Montague MP sent five pounds!

Many who were concerned about the lot of the poverty-stricken workers could only see them as an amorphous mass of subhuman creatures to be blamed or pitied, not as human beings with potential equal to their own; certainly not people one could invite to tea! Ben's eloquent letters must have shaken many of them, he had been born and bred among the poorest of the poor. When the upper class people met Ben and others like him they faced men often better read and informed than themselves.

During the latter half of 1887 meetings were held night after night throughout the whole dock area on both sides of the river and as far down as Tilbury. From huge Sunday morning meetings to small groups of men, discussing, learning, it was a campaign of education and a building up of the dock labourers' confidence in themselves.

It was only a small band of men who carried the campaign. Outstanding among them were Will Crooks and Tom McCarthy. Will Crooks had been building up for some years a tremendous following particularly in Poplar. He grasped the importance of the work among the labourers and although not a docker himself he put in all he had with Ben. He carried a small army with him, the many thousands who had listened to him week after week at his East India docks Sunday meetings.

Tom McCarthy was Ben's right hand man, he was the Secretary of one of the Stevedores Unions, a craft union not at that time in sympathy with the dock labourers. Whenever Tom was unable to get a morning's work, or had no immediate call to attend to from his own union, he was over to help. In his old age Ben remembered the comradeship of a host of men and women with affection; among them all there was a special place for Tom:

> Little Tom with his small square, straight backed figure, defiant head, and humorous face... his Irish spirit and indomitable courage were a source of inspiration in the struggle and for long he and I bore the main burden of speaking and organising.

1888

In the area around the Port of London, the greatest port in the British Empire, there was destitution. Men, women and children died of starvation. Skilled dockers were paid fourpence or fivepence an hour when work was available. Nothing when it was not.

There was a developing awareness and concern about the problem but few had an answer except to make some provision from charities and the Poor Law. Ben was thinking in different terms about what a great industry owed to its workers and how and when that debt should be paid. It was an industrial problem. Industry should solve it and would be healthier for doing so.

Men treated as responsible workmen, given good conditions and good equipment would earn, and should be paid, enough to support their families. The appeal was for justice not charity.

This was a different approach from that of H.M.

Hyndman and his Marxist class war. Different even from the idealistic Socialism of Robert Blatchford.

It was the basis on which Ben Tillett could call for support from all sections of the community.

Gas Workers and Match Girls

Ben took time off from his work for the dockers to help Will Thorne to form the Gas Workers Union, that was to become the National Union of Municipal Workers. The Gas Workers Union in 1888 won an extraordinary victory, the change from two 12-hour shifts every 24 hours to three 8-hour shifts.

In this same year Annie Besant arrived in the East End. She was one of the Fabian essayists who helped to formulate the principles on which Labour Party policies were to be formed in the years to come. She was not content with theory but took part in meetings and agitation. She held audiences spellbound with her eloquence and passion. In 1888 she took up the cause of the Bryant and May workers and led the seven hundred match girls in their successful strike against their appalling working conditions. The story of the gas workers and the match girls was news and widely published in the local and national press.

1889 the Stage is Set

Three factors now began to emerge:

PUBLIC OPINION: There were stirrings among Parliamentarians, the Press, and the public. Slumming became a West End pastime; the rich went down to docklands to see how the poor lived. The world's greatest centre of wealth, the City of London, was within a short walk of appalling squalor. The City now knew it.

STRATEGY: Ben had attended a lecture by a law student called Lang on the strategy and tactics of Napoleon's wars (Lang later went into the church and became Archbishop of Canterbury). Ben had for several years been considering the London dockers as one force, one army. Inspired by Napoleon's methods he had worked out routes for marches and lines of communication connecting every dock and wharf along both sides of the river. A total length of fifty miles. It was a unique plan for peaceful mobilisation.

FRIENDS: Friends were gathering around Ben Tillett's leadership:

Tom McCarthy	Secretary of the Society of Stevedores.
Ben Cooper	of the Cigar Makers Union.
Bill Steadman	of the Barge Builders Union.
Tom Mann	of the Amalgamated Society of Engineers.
John Burns	forceful outdoor speaker, also of the Engineers.

These and many more, although not one of them had the support of their unions and none of them was confident of success. It was a remarkable tribute to the small giant Ben Tillett that they went all the way with him in spite of their doubts. They knew he was right but doubted he could win.

From time to time Ben turned for help to his mentor, Cardinal Manning, whose understanding of the working man and the justice of his cause was a great source of strength. He chided Ben about some of his more violent speeches but softened his words on one occasion by adding, 'My dear Benjamin, if I was as young as you I'd do the same.' Ben described the Cardinal as 'a Saint of God.'

The stage was set.

Into Battle

On the evening of 12 August 1889 two members of the branch of the union that met in Wroots Coffee House, asked Ben to declare a strike at the South West India Dock. Ben was astonished. In the last two years he and his friends had met so much apathy, and at times hostility that he had expected that it would take more time before the men would have the confidence to act.

The dispute arose over the payment to the men on one particular cargo. Such disputes happened almost daily as the 'system' of payment was chaotic. Ben had already presented the men's case in writing to the employers. He had had no reply. It was agreed that he should present a series of demands to the Companies in person next morning and require an answer by twelve o'clock the next day.

The demands did not relate to just the immediate case but represented a first step towards the decasualisation of dock labour. The main points were:

> Wages to be raised to sixpence per hour.
> Overtime eightpence per hour.
> Employment to men to be at least four hours at a stretch.
> The contract system and piecework to be abolished.
> The number of call-ons to be reduced to two per day.

No one imagined for one moment that the obstinacy of the employers would evaporate overnight. It was a declaration of war.

It appeared to the employers that all they had to do was to sit back and watch the men starve and crawl back.

In later years Ben recalled his meetings with the Chairman of the Directors of the Dock Company, Mr. Norwood. He described Norwood as six feet high and weighing twenty stone, Ben was five feet four and weighed ten stone.

The meeting put the men's claims firmly on the table, but it was more a slanging match than a conference. Ben saw it with some humour as a David and Goliath situation. Had Norwood known his Bible as well as Ben he might have pondered on the fate of Goliath.

In his old age Ben remembered Norwood without bitterness; who else remembers him at all? What a chance that man missed; he could have been a pivotal figure in restructuring of British industry, a restructuring still to be achieved nearly one hundred years later. He was a small man.

Standstill

On an ordinary morning at the South West India Dock a crowd of dock labourers would be jostling and shouting desperately to be taken on for even an hour or two. On the morning of 14 August 1889 there was an empty dockside and an eerie silence. Dock labourers were casual workers, they had no service contracts to break, no rights, engaged by the hour, take it or leave it. They were determined not to work under those conditions again.

Ben knew that this could be a futile gesture. He knew that nothing less than bringing the whole Port of London to a standstill would achieve their aims. Ben knew that if they failed, if he failed, it would be years before such a brave effort could be mounted again.

Ben's long cherished plan was to reach every last man of the 100,000 workers in the Port of London with the message that they were going to come out together, march together, and win together. For this he needed 16,000 men to act as captains, lieutenants and sergeants to maintain contact and to organise small and large groups at every dock and wharf to maintain pickets, organise marches and meetings, see to relief tickets, head off blackleg labour and maintain morale. Within days this whole operation was underway and on 20 August 1889 the Port of London was closed.

No man worked and on old Father Thames scarcely a ship or barge moved. This was mute evidence to the solidarity of the Port workers that no one could ignore. Certainly not the City merchants looking out across the empty river and counting the cost, nor the Members of Parliament looking out from the Palace of Westminster. No doubt the old Queen was asking, 'What, Mr. Prime Minister, is going on?'

The Tasks and the Men

To get through the next few crucial days Ben needed to get four specific tasks performed. Each requiring a man of exceptional ability and dedication. In the event one task needed two men and all five completed their tasks brilliantly.

Three of these men accepted the challenge and walked ten feet tall alongside the Little Giant. The fourth doubted his ability to do what was needed, but he did. The fifth wore a uniform but disregarding precedent gave the same imaginative leadership as the others.

Tom McCarthy

The work in the Port of London involved many trades. The skilled men were organised in an array of small craft unions. Casual labourers were largely unorganised. There was no precedent for all the skilled tradesmen to support the dock labourers. Would they this time? The key was the two Stevedores Unions.

Tom McCarthy, Secretary of the Amalgamated Society of Stevedores, arrived on his own initiative at strike headquarters on the first morning, 14 August, offering his services. He had laid his job on the line, for his union had made no decision, but Tom had borne the brunt of the organising and speaking with Ben over the previous two years, he was not going to leave his side now.

The result of the Great Dock Strike of 1889 may well have turned on the action of this one man. Tom McCarthy, on the second day of the Strike, 15 August, arrived at the strike headquarters carrying, without permission, his union banner. That banner was carried at the head of the striking dockers in a great march that day to Tidal Basin, then on to Custom House, through much of the docks, and their numbers grew as others joined along the way. There was an improvised band to provide marching music and collection boxes out on either side to get the funds so urgently needed. In the next days, more bands, more marchers, more collectors and more banners, through every part of the docks. An army was on the march.

The stevedores were paid eightpence an hour to the dock labourers' fivepence. This was not their dispute, but on 18 August they issued a proclamation; they would stop work in support of the dock labourers. It was the breaking of a log jam. The first great task of winning support from the other unions had begun. They issued a proclamation:

Friends and Fellow-Workmen –

The dock labourers are on strike, and are asking for an advance in wages – the wages they now receive being 5d. per hour day time, and 6d. overtime. They now ask 6d. per hour day time and 8d. per hour overtime. The work is of the most precarious nature, three hours being the average amount per day obtained by the docker. We, the Union of Stevedores of London, knowing the conditions of the dock labourers, have determined to support their movement by every lawful means in our power. We have therefore refused to work because of the Dock Company employing scabs and blacklegs who are taking the place of the dock labourers on strike. We do this, not to inconvenience the brokers, shipowners, or master stevedores, as our quarrel is not with them, but we feel our duty is to support our poorer brothers. We are promised the help of the Seamen's and Firemen's Union, and we now appeal with confidence to members of all Trade Unions for joint action with us, and especially those whose work is in connection with shipping, seagoing engineers, boilermakers, ships' carpenters, painters and decorators, shipwrights, iron shipbuilders, caulkers, etc., etc., and also the coal heavers, ballastmen, lightermen, and their watchmen. We also appeal to the public at large for contributions and support on behalf of the dock labourers, which may be sent to Ben Tillett, Great Assembly Hall, Mile End Road; and in doing this we feel sure that our efforts will be appreciated – not as disturbers nor peace breakers, but as a demand from men determined to swerve not one inch from the attitude they have taken up, to succour the poor and uplift the downtrodden. On behalf of the United and Amalgamated Stevedores –

Thomas McCarthy,
T. M. Williams,
"Secretaries."

Tom Mann

The second task was to feed the one hundred thousand men of the docks and their families. On the first morning Ben sent a telegram to Tom Mann. Tom was not a dock worker but if there was a fight on for the workers he needed no second asking. Before midday he was down at strike headquarters; as the strike went on week by week he seemed to be everywhere at once, organising, encouraging, speaking at meetings. But when he first arrived Ben, no doubt remembering that Napoleon had said that 'an army marches on its stomach', put him in charge of the issue of relief tickets. It was an inspired move. Most of the strikers would have no money to buy food after the first few days. With a lesser man than Tom in charge it could have been disaster. Hardly had the relief tickets arrived from the printers than thousands of men crowded round the temporary headquarters at Wroots Coffee House. From the steps outside, Tom Mann appealed to them for order and discipline, every man would get a ticket. Then he set his back against one doorpost and jammed his foot against the opposite one. Every man had to crawl under his leg to get through the doorway. Inside, helpers gave out the tickets. Tom Mann held that position for several hours keeping everyone happy with cheery words and jokes. Feeding the 100,000 was underway.

In later years Ben was to find himself often in disagreement with Tom Mann's views and tactics but he remembered him with warmth and wit:

> His was the genius of sheer energy, his tremendous capacity for work became a mighty factor in the supreme crisis of the Dock Strike... sound at heart, self sacrificing and courageous, he has never deserted the flag, even if he has on occasion

attempted to plant it in impossible places.

On the morning of Sunday 18 August Ben called a mass meeting at the East India Dock gates. The Stevedores had agreed to attend and all the other unions with members in the docks had been invited. The platform was a wagon outside the dock gates, many thousands were present, and the collectors were busy. Ben Tillett spoke first followed by Tom Mann. It was common knowledge that the two Stevedores Unions were to call their men out, and this with the powerful speeches from the platform raised this huge mass of men to a pitch of enthusiasm. The Stevedores Union leaders issued their joint proclamation that day, the following day their men would not go to work.

Harry Orbell

Ben's speech on Sunday 18 August was for him just part of the day's work. Every section of the fifty mile front had to be manned and kept informed. The employers were circulating false stories that men were going back to work and they spared no expense to bring blackleg workers in from other parts of the country. The weakest point was the Tilbury Docks; not only were they cut off twenty miles down the river, remote from the daily morale-boosting meetings and processions but it was possible to by-pass the dock gates by taking imported workers straight into the docks by train. Ben asked the Christian lay preacher and great friend Harry Orbell to go down and take charge there. Harry Orbell had committed everything to the struggle; he had suffered victimisation and was unemployed and destitute. It was like promoting a reliable corporal to an independent command with the rank of colonel. The troops were untrained and unorganised, the outpost was difficult to defend and already under attack. Harry Orbell would have marched to his death leading a platoon but he could not see himself working out a strategy, allocating duties, or even looking like a leader of hundreds of men. But Ben seemed sure he was the man for the job, so off he went at once.

How Ben Tillett could handle men! He loved people, so he saw the full potential in a man. There is no other way of getting the best out of man woman or child. There is no other force that will bring unity.

Harry Orbell knew that the job was to keep the men confident and united and to thwart any tricks of the employers. Ben gave him no instructions as to how to do it, he was sure Harry Orbell was in his words 'designated by Providence to play the part that had to be played at Tilbury Docks.' So that was that.

Lay preacher Harry Orbell was now to practise what he preached, care for his men, do what needed to be done and trust the Lord. So he went among his men keeping their spirits up by his own cheerful confidence. He arranged a system of travelling pickets who gave out leaflets and talked to the imported workmen on the trains, exposing the true state of affairs, explaining the lies they had been told to get them from other ports. Many decided not to damage the strike, left the trains and returned home.

On one occasion Harry Orbell decided to intercept a train load of workmen being brought in from Liverpool. With a group of his men he waited beneath an embankment near the north gate of the dock until the train drew near and slowed down; then they swarmed over the rails and actually began to push the train back.

The imported workmen left the train and returned home at their own expense.

Harry Orbell's intelligence service enabled him to anticipate all the employers' tricks; among these was a report that the strike was over at Tilbury and men were needed to catch up arrears of work. On another occasion the employers actually went to the expense of dressing up a large number of strike-breakers with black coats and walking sticks, like city business men.

The dock owners and their managers were out-thought and out-fought by that man of faith Harry Orbell and his merry men. Tilbury, from being a lonely outpost, became a shining beacon to the whole of docklands.

John Burns

If there was a fight on for the rights of the workers in those days John Burns would be there in the front line. So he joined up with the dock labourers although he had been sceptical of their chances. John Burns was his own man, like Tom Mann a member of the respectable craft union the Amalgamated Society of Engineers, where the members' political stance was more Liberal than Socialist. He was still a member of the Marxist Social Democratic Federation, but at the same time in his speeches he spoke of sound homes and sobriety in a manner that would do credit to a Methodist lay preacher. He was proud of his craft, wanted to replace the greed and selfishness of capitalism with a new order and saw that the way men lived was basic to achieving his vision. These things did not seem to him incompatible; they were parts of the one whole. Added to all this he was an extrovert character with a voice like thunder, and a capacity for work to match Ben Tillett and Tom Mann.

John Burns, the fourth key man, was to take on the organising of the daily marches often leading them himself. They were to march through the City to Tower Hill on Monday 19 August. This was a vital task. The march would rally and strengthen the dock workers and would demonstrate that here was a force that could not be ignored or denied.

There was a menacing cloud overhanging the proposed marches, indeed over the whole enterprise. The forces of law and order feared large assemblies of workers. In this case there were one hundred thousand men, many of them illiterate and hungry, surely a threat to the very fabric of society. Many in authority would see it as their duty to stop them from entering the City of London. The Government had troops on stand-by. There were memories of the 'Peterloo Massacre' in 1819 when mounted yeomanry and soldiers charged a large demonstration in Manchester and eleven were killed and hundreds injured. Only two years before in 1887 a march of the unemployed to Trafalgar Square became known as 'Bloody Sunday' as a result of a head-on clash with the police. Was not that man John Burns at the head of that one too?

Superintendent Forster

The march went ahead on Monday 19 August. The people crowding the pavement and watching from their office windows could not believe their eyes. Yes, there was indeed that man John Burns at the head but marching beside him was Superintendent Forster of the City of London police. Could anything be more unlikely than the white straw hat of Burns and the helmet of Forster side by side?

Ben Tillett and John Burns in the midst of their avalanche of tasks had failed to ask permission to march through the City. This was a bad mistake; they had put themselves in the wrong. Forster could have sat tight, waited for the men to march and thrown barriers of his men across every approach to the City, with his mounted officers in reserve, and fought it out. Most men in his position would have done just that as they did at Peterloo and on Bloody Sunday.

The situation called for a man of courage. Forster was the man. Being a good policeman he would have known who had been taking leadership in the area these last years, Ben Tillett, Will Crooks, Tom McCarthy, Harry Orbell. He knew what was in the wind and he went to see Tillett and Burns and he gave them permission to march. It was a triumph for democracy by the marching men and one man in uniform who guaranteed in his own person their right to march.

The Companies were angry and were foolish enough to issue a furious attack on the police; they had been hoping that policemen's truncheons would do what they had failed to do, break the dockers' spirit.

Some historical records omit the part played by Superintendent Forster; he even got his name spelled two different ways. Ben Tillett remembered him all his life; his own words were 'the Superintendent remained throughout the strike one of our best friends.' Had he not filled the role that he did the vanguard of the men would have met his police in the narrow streets of the City with thousands more men funnelling in from the rear. It would have made the Peterloo massacre look like a minor skirmish.

Marching Men

So on the first Monday of the Great Dock Strike thousands of dock labourers marched through the City of London — dock labourers, stevedores, shore gangs, lightermen, painters, riggers, carmen, firemen, scalers, ironworkers and lumpers. There were some fine official banners and others mere old rags, fish heads and pieces of rotten meat on poles and effigies of the undersized children of the poor. There were carts carrying representations of the gear used by the dockers and stevedores. Along the route men poured out from the congested slums of courts and alleys and joined in the march. On Tower Hill a mass meeting was held and it was announced that a dockers' union had been formed.

The audacity, scale and discipline of it all was sensational. It announced to the dock companies, to Parliament, press and people and to the City that there was a new force to be reckoned with in the land. No one was more surprised than the men themselves. A minor strike of a handful of labourers had grown into something approaching a disciplined army in four days.

Ben Tillett with Tom McCarthy and a few others had been working for two years building up the confidence of the dock workers that their circumstances could be changed. They had spoken at hundreds of meetings large and small. Others, particularly Will Crooks, had been carrying on a crusade of morale boosting and educational meetings. They had created a ground swell.

The whole concept had only ever existed in the head of one man, Ben Tillett; the theme was good communications and marching men. There was no organisation to which 100,000 men belonged. Far from it. Very few of the casual labourers belonged to a union, while membership of many of the craft unions ran to only three figures rather than four. These small unions were managed by unpaid committee men in their spare time after a long hard day's work. Ben Tillett had been humping tons of tea up and down the stairs of a tea warehouse up until the day the strike began.

On every day of the strike the men from the Port of London marched to meetings on Tower Hill or in Hyde Park. History records no violence. Meanwhile the Directors of the Companies made no move to meet the men while cargoes rotted at the quayside.

A Strike Committee had emerged consisting of Tillett, Burns, Mann and McCarthy. To these were added Toomey of the Stevedores, H.H. Champion a journalist and representatives of the various unions as they formally joined the strike. The Committee met every day with such members as could attend. All of them were active in the field organising marches, meetings and relief work, dealing with local crises and for some attending to their own union business.

The plan was colossal in its conception, but the message was simple, 'The whole Port of London is coming out - that means you.' Some were quick to respond and local union officials and active union members took up the call along with the huge numbers of unorganised casual labourers. Some at first did not believe what they heard, but had to believe what they saw. The marching men with bands and banners, sometimes the head of John Burns appearing over a dock wall as he stood on the backs of other men and his huge voice roared out challenging them to join the march, not next week, not tomorrow but now.

The whole secret was the march; this was a movement that moved. Napoleon's secret was the mobility of his armies. When he was at last brought to a halt outside Moscow he was lost. Two world wars have taught us the value of movement and the tragedy of the static army.

Every man working in the London docks was being given the opportunity to see for himself and to be seen as part of an irresistible force 100,000 strong.

Comrades in Arms

Everybody in the Port of London now knew the young man Ben Tillett. Men in the Craft Unions had begun to respect his oratory and conviction, although up to now few had believed in his vision of creating trade unionists out of casual labourers, still less the possibility of getting the Craft Unions to march with them. Suddenly they saw the dream becoming a reality before their eyes.

The break through with the Stevedores was quickly followed as others began to lead their men into the fray behind the small giant who had emerged from nowhere in two short years. Bill Steadman, a marvellous Cockney character from the Barge Builders Union, later a member of the LCC and a MP; Harry Kay who later became the Treasurer of the new Dockers Union; T.M. Williams, Secretary of the United Stevedores; T.M. Walsh of the Sailors and Firemens Union; G. Miller of the East London Painters Union; Ben Cooper, Secretary of the Cigar Makers Union; Will Thorne of the Gas Workers Union repaid Ben for his help in the previous year; members of the Watermen and Lightermen and the Crane Drivers Union; Harry Quelch who did great work in organising the South Bank; and hundreds more.

Many years later Ben could recite their names like a roll of honour. But the honour was his for his vision and his extraordinary capacity to appreciate the potential in everyone. Such diverse personalities, representing every section in the Christian Church and every brand of Socialist, he saw the best in them all and remembered with warmth and affection even some who in later years undercut the unity that he had worked so hard to achieve.

He did not forget the vital part the women played in those days.

Mrs. Toomey, wife of James Toomey of the Stevedores, provided meals at all hours in their little house not five minutes walk from Headquarters. He described Mrs. Hickey presiding at 'Wade's Arms' as 'that great Irish soul who became the hub of the universe.' Of his own wife he wrote, 'My best friend and colleague. During the years of tumult she was not only a steadfast wife, but was assistant secretary of the Union founded in 1887 at the Oak Tavern Inn, Hackney. She was the mother of the Dockers Union, and a mighty comrade.'

He remembered Annie Besant who arrived in the East End to write about the poor and stayed to lead the Match Girls' strike of 1888. With her spirited voice, eloquence and passion she made quite an impact when she spoke at some of Ben's meetings. He remembered Beatrice Potter who also made and published a first hand investigation into the lives of the East End workers and in later years with her husband Sidney Webb played such a great part in the Labour Movement. The 1889 strike was fought against a growing background of knowledge of how the poor lived and died.

Many of the clergy who had lived alongside the dock workers and supported them in all the hardships that they had to endure stood by Ben now. The Rev. J.G. Adderley in charge of the Christ Church Mission in Poplar raised £800. The clergy at Toynbee Hall raised money and helped with the relief as did Canon Barnett and the Baptists Rev. John Wilson and the Rev. J.C. Carlisle and many others.

The Times of 4 September 1889 reported:

> Last night a densely crowded meeting was held in the Bermondsey Town Hall for the purpose of obtaining 'help for the sufferers through the strike...' The Rev. J.C. Carlisle moved the first resolution — 'That this meeting heartily sympathises with the dock labourers of London in their strike for the moderate and reasonable increase in their pay, and urges them to remain firm and united till their joint demands are conceded.'

The Times of 5 September reported:

> At the Salvation Army's depot in the Whitehall Road... 9,000 loaves were consumed by those on strike in one day, the West India Dock Road depot was carrying out an even larger relief operation...'

The Times of 7 September reported:

> The Rev. C.H. Kelly, President of the Wesleyan Conference was present at the ninth free breakfast given to men on strike at St. George's Wesleyan Mission, Cable Street yesterday morning. A free breakfast is provided for 700 men each day and at 1 o'clock women and children receive free dinners for their families. At the breakfast the Wesleyan President congratulated the men on their good behaviour.... He assured the strikers of the sympathy of the tens of thousands of Methodists all over the land.

I asked my Aunt Mary when she was one hundred years old if she remembered the Dock Strike. This was a very long shot as she would have been only four years old; talking with Aunt Mary was rather like a lucky dip. This was my lucky day; she answered at once. It was down by where the Woolwich Ferry docked; Ellie (her elder sister) had got some of the dockers to sit down on the steps there, she had made some tea or soup in a sort of tub and she ladled it out into mugs for them. Ellie, my mother, was fourteen years old at the time.

The Great Dock strike of 1889 was a whole community rising in revolt against a repulsive system that denied them the basic necessities of life.

Read All About It

Never had there been such a widely publicised dispute. Newspaper men representing the London and provincial Press and from many foreign newspapers crowded into the Strike Headquarters every day. Young Fleet Street reporter Tom Marlowe was a regular attender; years later he became the Editor of the *Daily Mail* and the head of the Northcliffe Press. T.P. O'Conner, Editor of the *London Evening Star*, was a staunch ally and along with *Pall Mall Gazette*, the *Labour Elector* and other papers helped the fund raising. It was after all a pressman's dream, larger than life characters, action every day, frequent handouts in the form of manifestos, leaders completely accessible, no closed doors. With the Port of London at a standstill and tens of thousands of men marching even the most unsympathetic paper could not ignore what was going on.

Henry Hyde Champion, a Socialist journalist who founded the *Labour Elector*, took charge of briefing the press along with Tillett and Burns. Champion was an interesting character, university educated, son of a major general and himself a former artillery officer. He knew something about marching too.

Wrong Move

By the end of August after two and a half weeks of marches and meetings every day the strike was still holding. But now the fund-raising efforts on the daily marches and the collections from organisations and individuals were not producing enough. The situation was desperate.

The Committee met, with Burns, Mann and Champion among those present, and decided to send a manifesto calling on all London workers to join the strike on Monday 2 September, unless the employers met the dockers' demands. Ben Tillett had dashed off to deal with a 'back to work' move among wharf labourers at Wapping and so was not present at the meeting. Late at night and tired out after dealing with that situation he had gone home to bed. At two o'clock in the morning Tom Mann got him up to sign the manifesto. He signed and accepted responsibility for doing so, but in the light of day he knew it was a blunder.

The Strike Committee had no right to call on trade union members working outside the Port of London. It had been done over the heads of the unions concerned without any consultation. It was constitutionally wrong and would not succeed. Ben got to work to repair the damage. He drafted a new manifesto cancelling the call to extend the strike and won the support of Burns, Mann, Toomey, McCarthy and the rest of the Committee. This was an example of his wisdom and authority. The new manifesto was read out at the usual Hyde Park meeting on Sunday 1 September.

Aussies Save the Day

On the same day on the other side of the world the Brisbane wharf labourers met and decided to send help. This by itself would not have been remarkable; some support had already come in from many parts of the world. For some reason, never fully explained, this action by the Brisbane men released a floodgate of contributions not only from dockers but from every section of the Australian people. The banks remitted money without charge. The Postmaster General sent cables free. The Salvation Army sent the profits from *War Cry*. Football clubs telegraphed their gate money. Every union sent donations, commonly in three figures. The subscriptions began to arrive in London, first in single amounts, then in a growing shower until the Australian gifts reached the fantastic sum of £30,000.

The dockers were now organised, disciplined, confident in their leader and determined to get all that they had fought for.

The Directors of the Dock Companies were appalled at any suggestion that they should recognise or do any sort of deal with the dock labourers. The shipowners wanted a settlement and some even considered by-passing the dock owners and employing their own labour. Wharfingers were prepared to offer concessions to men at their own wharf and some did.

The Lord Mayor, Alderman James Whitehead, called together some leading citizens to mediate on the dispute. The group included Cardinal Manning, the Bishop of London (Dr. Temple), Lord Brassey, Sir John Lubbock MP (President of the London Chamber of Commerce), Alderman Sir Andrew Lusk, and Mr. Sydney Buxton MP. The Lord Mayor asked the dockers' leaders to meet them. The first proposal put to Tillett and Burns was that there should be an immediate return to work and that in return there should be a negotiated increase in wages to take effect on 1 March. The Directors wanted to give themselves time to negotiate increased charges with the ship owners that would cover the cost of the wage increases. This proposal was rejected out of hand.

A more radical proposal was later put to the dockers, that included acceptance of the sixpence an hour wage with eightpence an hour overtime but commencing on 1 January. Ben Tillett and John Burns put the proposal to a mass meeting of the dockers in Hyde Park and it was rejected.

One member of the Committee stood apart, Cardinal Manning, he now committed himself wholly to bringing about a settlement. He spent day after day at the Mansion House meeting members of the Committee, representatives of the Dock Directors and Tillett and Burns, listening, discussing, persuading. Eighty years of age, a man with great authority in the Church but none here except the authority of his own integrity and compassion. He understood the hardships and injustice that society imposed on the casual labourers and their families and had supported the Methodist lay preacher Joseph Arch, 20 years before in his fight for the Agricultural Workers.

He met with 'Goliath' Norwood and the Dock Directors and urged them to reconsider the position. The dockers were united, well organised and determined, they had extensive public support. What would happen next if they became convinced that discipline and restraint would not move the Directors? The alternative of violence had been known in London in recent years but never employed by such a force as this. He left them to face reality as they had not done up to now. He went away to produce a practical proposal.

Meanwhile the daily battle to keep up the morale of the vast army of strikers and their families went on. At a meeting on 9 September on Tower Hill John Burns spoke once more to a huge crowd; he was brilliant as ever after four weeks of non-stop effort. He made the famous speech in which he used the image of the garrison at Lucknow straining eyes to catch the first glimpse of the relieving bayonets. 'This, lads, is the Lucknow of Labour, and I myself, looking to the horizon, can see a silver gleam not of bayonets to be imbued in a brother's blood, but the gleam of the full round orb of the dockers' tanner.' Perhaps he believed it, perhaps it was a last desperate throw to hold those hungry men for just a few more days for the gleam to become a reality, conscious that if it did not, all hell would break loose.

Turning Point

The dockers made an inspired move and asked Cardinal Manning to meet the full Strike Committee the following day 10 September. The meeting took place in a school class-room in Kirby Street, Poplar. When Manning arrived he insisted on shaking hands with each member of the Committee and learnt their names. They had his proposals before them; they would get their sixpence an hour and eightpence for overtime but some of their demands would be deferred. He wanted to hear from Ben Tillett first, he knew that he would oppose acceptance of those terms, and he did. Ben had never put forward any wild claims, the dockers' claims were fair and modest, such as any reasonable man would accept. Now he was feeling in his bones the years of deprivation. He did not want to give way. Everyone present recognised the depth of his feelings and the justification for them, no one more than Manning himself. They met for four hours; in the end it was the sheer love that Manning had for these men that cancelled out their bitterness. They knew that he understood. He had fought long and hard with the Company Directors and he understood them too. So they agreed. Had bitterness directed their decision they would have continued the strike probably to defeat and possibly to violence and disaster.

So Manning, this frail and saintly man, left them to gather his strength to overcome the resistance of the Directors.

The Times of 13 September reported:

> The directors held yesterday a protracted conference with the Cardinal Archbishop of Westminster. The Cardinal is now generally recognised to be holding out the olive-branch in the form of the proposed November settlement.... Should the men be induced to make this offer and to abide by it, and should it be accepted, Cardinal Manning will have performed an immense feat.

The basis of the settlement was to be sixpence an hour and eightpence for overtime, with a minimum of 4 hours pay once taken on. There was to be no victimisation. A joint committee of employers and men was to be set up to settle details.

Ben had to gather his strength as he stood on the top of a hansom cab and with a voice hoarse with exhaustion battled to persuade a mass meeting down by the West India Dock to accept the terms. He needed all his power and eloquence to argue the case and silence some noisy and hostile elements.

John Burns read out the terms of the settlement and during the meeting had to read them out twice more. The vote for agreement was overwhelmingly carried. The crowd broke up, unharnessed the horse, and drew the cab with Ben Tillett and John Burns through the streets to the 'Wade's Arms.'

Victory

On 16 September the men returned to work preceded on Sunday the 15th by a triumphant march to Hyde Park. Llwellyn Smith and Vaughan Nash, who wrote a report of the strike, described it:

All along Commercial Road, the women turned out in thousands to see their husbands and their sons pass in triumph. The sun seemed brighter, the music more inspiring, the banners more in number than ever before; and never in any one Sunday procession had so many actual dockers walked together. There was a holiday look about them, and all seemed fresher and tidier than was their wont. Benjamin Tillett and John Burns took the lead as usual, in a space jealously cleared by the marshals. Tillett in his Sunday best, was devouring the newspapers, while Burns seemed to be making notes for his final speech, and now and then roused himself to eject an intruder from the sacred space, or to burst through the crowd and buy a few pennyworth of plums at a costermonger's stall. All the usual emblems were there, Neptune and his suite, Britannia wrapped in her Union Jack, Macaulay on the ladder. Scarcely one of the old familiar features of the five weeks' processions was missing from the great triumphal march. On went the procession with good swinging step to the sound of the 'Marseillaise' and 'Rule Britannia', the latter with a big drum accompaniment that left no doubt of the intention of the marching Britons, never, never to be slaves again. The stirring marching music gave place to the more rollicking strains of 'He's a Jolly Good Fellow' as the processionists halted before the Mansion House, and dipped their flags and cheered the Lord Mayor and Lady Mayoress who were espied on the balcony.

On they went through Queen Victoria Street, to the Thames Embankment, but the sun was shining fiercely now and the men were getting fagged, so a halt was cried at Westminster Palace, when its fairy skyline came in sight. Banners were laid on the hard baked ground, or propped against the parapet of the Embankment, and the weary crowd found seats on the low granite walls, or loafed about eating such lunch as they had brought. The luckier patronised the ginger beer and plums of enterprising costermongers. The police had been prepared for the halt, and producing their lunch, ate it in all good fellowship with the processionists. Father Neptune and his suite dismounted from their trolley and trailed off regardless of dignity, to the nearest eating house.

At 2 o'clock the order was given to fall in again, and the procession wound on, with its accompanying fringe of open-eyed boys and curious spectators, through Victoria Street and Hyde Park Corner, a spot that had seen the beginning of so many Labour movements, and had celebrated the triumph of so few. Four platforms were erected in the Park, but none attracted so much attention as the first at which John Burns and Tillett were to speak. Fiery Tom McCarthy presided, but there were no fiery words today; only mutual congratulation on the victory that had been won. It was a picnic rather than a fighting demonstration.

John Burns spoke from three platforms. The tone of all three speeches was the same. Gratitude to friends, moderation in the hour of triumph, forgetfulness of bygones, hope for the future. Ben Tillett's speech was one of the best he had made throughout the strike. The note he struck was the value of Union to the men, and the absolute necessity of keeping the word they had pledged. Some men had been hesitating about returning to work, but they must all go in on Monday morning. A voice was heard. 'How about the blacklegs?' Never mind the blacklegs, he replied, everyone who has been on strike must return to work in the morning, if – and here his words became slower and more emphatic – you have any respect for your leaders or for yourselves.

After the strike the new Dock Wharf Riverside and General Workers Union, with Ben Tillett as General Secretary had 30,000 members.

The arrival of the 'New Unions' as the unions of dockers and other labourers were called and the single event of the Dock Strike stimulated recruitment in all sections of workers.

In 1886 the Trade Unions affiliated to the Trade Union Congress had in all 500,000 members. In 1890 they had 1,600,000 members. It was a turning point.

Ben Tillett's birthday was 11 September; I wonder if

anyone remembered it. He was twenty-nine. Few men have ever crowded as much into a lifetime as he had crowded into those twenty-three years since he had worked in the brickyard as a child.

Ben Tillett after several unsuccessful attempts was elected a Member of Parliament in 1917 and held the seat in 1918, 1922 and 1923. In 1929 he was President of the Trade Union Congress. He served as General Secretary of the Dockers Union continuously for thirty-four years until 1923. It had by then become the Transport and General Workers Union.

Ben Tillett is remembered as the man who led a great strike and changed the working conditions of a whole industry, but he himself was proud to say that of the thousands of disputes in which he was involved in later years the proportion that were settled without a stoppage was 500 to 1. The achievement was the measure of his strength and skill but even more of his warmth and humanity. He has been described as 'achieving more than any other single person for the welfare of the workers.' As he lay, in his old age, close to death he said he would like to give his comrades a last message. It was printed the following Sunday in *Reynolds News*:

> The Trade Union Movement should stand for more than wages and sordid commercialism. It must develop a soul if it is to do its job of uplifting humanity.

Drink

Alcohol is man's oldest drug. Moderate drinking has been justified because it helps man to relax after a day's work, to release inhibitions in social relations, to blot out life's disasters. This is one side of the picture; the other side is excess drinking leading to the neglect of the family and social responsibilities and to disruption and violence.

A doctor in a report that had the support of the British Research Council described moderate drinking:

> Without signs of intoxication in the full or legal sense of the term, the bearing and individual attitude of mind suffer temporary change as an effect of the drug; and those in contact with the person so affected have for the time being to deal with an altered individual, whose mind lacks temporarily its normal factor of judgement and conspicuous elements of self-control.

In the light of this clinical description of moderate drinking, how do we stop this 'altered individual' from becoming drunk? And how do we protect the rest of society from his, often disgusting, behaviour when he is drunk? Are we justified in restricting the freedom of the many because of the anti-social behaviour of the few? Babylonian law in 1770 BC regulated drinking houses and governments have done so ever since. In this country statutes of Edward IV in 1552 gave the local justices power to restrict the sale of intoxicating drink to premises that they licensed. Four hundred Acts of Parliament later we continue the principle of licences for the sale of alcoholic drink, restrict opening hours and the sale of alcohol to children and so on. Penal taxation increases, although whether the motive behind this is to put a brake on sales or just to increase revenue is arguable. Successive governments grapple with the problem; as I write the issues are teenage drinking, football crowds, and the drink factor in violent crime and death on the roads.

Alcohol and the Poor

In Victorian times all who cared about the condition of the poor were concerned about the 'demon drink.' In the overcrowded industrial towns and cities most workers lived near the poverty line. Every penny spent on drink was a penny needed for food or fuel or basic clothing for the family. Yet as an escape from the drab misery of their lives many of the poorest turned to drink.

Take the dock worker. In the early morning often before day had dawned, in the cold and wet he herded with his fellow workers at the dockside to take his chance for a few hours work. If he failed, he hung around for the next call. If he got only a few hours work he waited, hoping for more. He was paid by the hour or even half-hour. A docker might spend half his life waiting and half working. There were beer houses at every corner. The temptation for a warm and a pint was powerful. He did not need the preacher, the magistrate or anyone else to tell him what a wicked stupid fellow he was to spend his hard earned fivepence an hour on beer. He knew all this perfectly well when he faced his wife and family at the end of the day.

It was easy to blame him. Who would help him? Not every church would welcome him, but there were two groups who would hold out the hand of friendship to him, drunk or sober, the Salvation Army and the Temperance Movement; their members were out on the streets looking for people like him. Their solution to his problem was that he would 'sign the pledge' never to drink again, and that they would stand by him and with God's help see him through. Tens of thousands accepted the challenge; my mother's father was one of them.

Staff Commander Frederick Townshend RN was master of a squadron's flagship, the HMS Narcissus. One dark wet night in 1874 they hove to off Palermo on the Admiral's orders. Townshend left two lieutenants in charge on deck and retired to his bunk; he had been on deck for three days and two nights piloting the ship between the Greek islands. That night the ship drifted ashore. They got her off next day, with little damage.

Townshend along with other officers was court marshalled, he was found guilty of hazarding the ship and sentenced to lose two years seniority. This incident should have ended there but for the curious action of the Admiralty; they quashed his sentence on a technicality but dismissed him from his ship. He was only forty-one years of age but his naval career was in tatters.

In bitterness and despair he took to drink and was dismissed from the navy as being 'unfit for further service.'

He returned to his home in Woolwich and drank away all his savings. On one occasion he received one hundred pounds in prize money. He spent it in the pubs of Woolwich, putting a sovereign on the bar and ordering drinks all round. He was king of Woolwich for a fortnight.

One night he was picked up by the Salvation Army and taken to their 'citadel.' While they sang a hymn he signed the pledge. He never drank again.

Total Abstinence

The Temperance Movement in its broadest sense included all the great religions of the world. Total abstinence was the rule for most Christian denominations, Methodists, Baptists, Quakers and others. The Church of England while not making total abstinence a rule had a strong Temperance Society founded in 1862. It included Archbishops and Bishops who practised and advocated total abstinence themselves. The other great religions Muslim, Buddhist, Hindu all embraced total abstinence as an article of faith. The millions across the world who turned to God, turned away from alcohol. They did not have to 'give up' something for which they had never seen the need.

The Good Templars

Many active Christians felt the need to form an organisation to fight for an alcohol-free world, to take up the political and legal aspects of controlling the sale of alcohol, to educate men, women and children on the dangers of drink, and to support the reformed alcoholic.

The Pilgrim Fathers who sailed to America to find a new life were Free Church total abstainers and it was natural that the largest temperance organisation 'The International Order of Good Templars' was founded in America in 1851. By 1897 the Order had 391,600 members organised in 9,575 lodges across the world; 104,796 of these members were in the United Kingdom.

The Good Templars became a major force in Britain, not just because of its size but because of the thorough way its members were trained. The lodge was small and local with usually thirty or forty members. They saw themselves as being in a battle for the health and happiness of the nation. They studied what alcohol was, how alcoholic drinks were made and the effect they had. They studied the licensed trade and the law relating to it. All the members took examinations! They had speakers on many subjects at their meetings and learned to speak themselves by taking part in the meetings and, surprisingly, playing games. They made music. They met on serious business but their weekly meetings were happy social occasions, eagerly looked forward to, and never missed.

There was an organisation for the children called 'The Band of Hope' that was on the same scale as the adult movement. When adults and children got together in one of their great family festivals they did things in style. In London the whole Crystal Palace and grounds used to be taken over annually for a day. For the 1883 festival there was a senior and junior choir each of 5,000 voices and a total attendance of 66,957.

The Licensed Trade

The Good Templars needed all their training to do battle with the licensed trade, for although there were individual publicans who kept a respectable house, the trade was a powerful antagonist. One example shows the way they often completely ignored the social consequences of the way the trade was conducted. In the year 1900 the Oldham justices issued a recommendation that young children should not be served with beer. The reaction of the Oldham and District Licensed Victuallers and the Beer, Wine and Spirit Trade Association was to issue a circular that read, in part, as follows:

> Stand firm, continue to serve children as formerly, except very young children, say under six or seven years of age, if it is advisable that they should not be supplied.

Women

The Good Templars were concerned not just about alcohol; they were concerned about the quality of life for everyone. When my mother was elected chairman of the 'Lily of the Vale' Lodge No 3635 in 1903 a woman chairman was not unusual in the Good Templars but would be inconceivable anywhere else. The rule read:

> ELIGIBILITY: Male and female are admitted and are on a perfect equality as to eligibility for office etc.

Colour

In 1853 James R. Jones, a black man, was elected a representative of his lodge to visit the Grand Lodge of America. He hesitated about going, afraid that he would not be received; but a white representative A.M. Tombs urged him to go saying, 'If you are not received, they don't receive me either....' James R. Jones was in fact received without question. However the colour question rumbled on and in 1864 the Chief Templar Samuel D. Hastings felt the need to lay down the line again and wrote in his report:

> The Bible reveals the fact... that God hath made of one blood all nations of men to dwell upon the face of the earth... all mankind are equally the object of his love and care.

A question about colour was answered by an officer of the Good Templars in 1868 with these immortal words:

> Proceed in all cases as though they were white. I do not understand that our Order takes into account the colour of a man's skin any more than it does the colour of his hair or eyes.

They were brave words in America in 1868, as they would have been anywhere in the British Empire at that time.

Religion

It had been taken for granted that the Good Templars was a Christian organisation, but in 1881 came another challenge; the Grand Lodge of India asked permission to use Hindu prayers and scriptures instead of Christian prayers and the Bible. The World Lodge meeting refused, declaring the divinity of Christ to be a fundamental principle of the Order. We must not be too hard on the Good Templars of over one hundred years ago when Christians dismissed all non-Christians as 'heathen.' It was a sad decision born of the prejudices of the whole society in which they lived. They had bravely challenged current attitudes on the rights of women and the rights of the blacks. Now here were these brown people with ancient religious beliefs held as deeply as their own. In 1906 on the recommendation of an Englishman, Joseph Malins, then the world leader of the Good Templars, the World Lodge reversed their decision and agreed that their brothers and sisters in India should use their Hindu prayers and scriptures. This was not a wishy-washy decision made by people who were unsure of their own faith; it was made by men and women who had grasped

the heart of the teaching of Jesus. He turned no one away
and nor would they.

LILY OF THE VALE LODGE, 3635.

(Sub-District, No. 3.)

V.D., Bro. Skelton.

St. John's Schools, Welling-
ton Street, Woolwich.

Wednesdays, 8 o'clock.

D.G.C.T. Sis. (Miss) Townshend,
61A, Station-road, Plumstead.

The Good Templars was the nursery of many Labour
pioneers. It was where Keir Hardie met his wife Lily,
where my father met my mother, where they and
thousands like them learnt to speak up for what they
believed.

W. Moncrieff, D.C.T.

DISTRICT LODGE SESSION.

Will Lodge Deputies please read the
following at the next Two Sessions
of their Lodges.

The 131st QUARTERLY
SESSION of District
Lodge will be held on
SATURDAY, NOV. 18,
1905, in the Foresters'
Hall, Raglan Road,
Forest Hill.

110

Clarion Call

Robert Blatchford, one of the highest paid journalists of his day, spent several months in 1890 on a survey of the Manchester slums. He found not a small enclave of 'drop-outs', but a vast area where up to sixty thousand workers lived where there was not one decent habitation. He wrote, 'poverty there was and wretchedness to make the heart ache.' Concerned that no one would believe his story he took the owner of the paper Mr. (later Sir) Edward Hutton to see for himself. He described one visit. 'The husband had just died of consumption; his body was laid out on the kitchen table. There was no fire and no bed. Three young children cowered together on the floor with a couple of sacks over them, and the widow sat on an empty box crying herself blind.'

Blatchford began to write not only about the horrors of the slums but also of the hope of a new society that he called socialism. His socialism was not rooted in intellectual economic theory, or in the class war. Not to be achieved 'come the revolution' or 'when we get to Heaven' but a way of life to be lived now. Out of this living would emerge a new society where every need would be met and every man, woman and child would have the chance to give their best.

His Editor gave him the choice to stop writing this

Socialist stuff or get out. He got out. He founded his own weekly newspaper in 1891.

It was called *The Clarion*. He owned it with a small group of friends, and edited it under the name of Nunquam. My father bought a copy of No. 1 when he was thirteen years old; a boy grew up fast in those days, by then he had been at work for three years. In later years, after my father married in 1903, Robert Blatchford often stayed in our home. They kept in touch right up to my father's death in 1930.

The Clarion had a magazine-like format and carried analyses of industrial and social problems, with facts and statistics eagerly quarried as material for speeches by men like my father. There were articles and columns on the theatre and entertainment, education and sport. A.M. Thompson, who was fluent in French and German and had lived through the Commune of Paris in 1871, wrote on European affairs. It was rich with wit and humour. Above all it exposed the evil in society and described a Socialist alternative that the working men could understand and apply.

A nationwide movement of *Clarion* readers sprang up without central direction or control, the Rt. Hon. J.R. Clynes gives the flavour of it:

> The name of the paper was proudly linked with active and mobile Scouts — The Fellowship, Travelling Vans, Clubs, Choirs, Cycling Groups and Clarion Meets. The Meets were meetings of delight to those who travelled to them, and drowsy places in the country and old market towns were aroused and instructed by able speakers who carried a message to remote quarters where a Socialist voice had never previously been heard. If a Meet could not be organised because a place was too small a Clarion van would go to the place and the speaker with it. By such means scores of villages

were visited, leaflets given and pamphlets and *Clarions* sold to the startled but friendly folks of rural England. The Clubs were living centres for educational debates and for organising meetings and social gatherings. The choirs attracted great crowds and succeeded where posters failed. All these varied activities aroused interest, set people talking thinking and reading.... We do not forget the splendid record of a paper unique in the life of Labour journalism and not surpassed in its time by any single effort to make socialists who would be conscious of their faith and make Labour folks in quality and numbers fit to rule their country.

I was sitting with my elder brother in his home in Folkestone; he was eighty years old, I was four years younger. I was trying to bring his memory to the aid of mine. 'John', I said, 'there are all these heads, hundreds I think, I am a little above them. Away in the distance is some box-like shape, I can't describe it, and there is a man standing on it speaking. Someone says "that's your Dad".' John replied at once, 'That's a *Clarion* caravan, mother is at the back of the crowd holding you up in her arms. Dad is speaking. You would be no more than two years old.' That is my earliest memory of any kind. Millions of people remember *The Clarion*. It shaped their lives. It shaped my father's life, and through his, mine.

Merrie England

Robert Blatchford wrote one series of twenty-seven pieces in *The Clarion* in the form of letters to a Mr. John Smith; these he put together as a book called *Merrie England*. I have a tattered copy of the cheap edition beside me; it is dated 1894, it is just over two hundred pages. In large letters on the front cover is the price 'ONE PENNY' for its 204 pages.

Merrie England sold over one million copies in Britain alone, probably more in America. There were translations into Dutch, German, Spanish, Danish and other languages.

It begins:

> Dear Mr. Smith, I am sorry to hear that you looked upon Socialism as a vile and senseless thing, and upon Socialists as wicked or foolish men.... I mean to argue the point with you.... You entertain a wholesome contempt for theories and have a habit of calling 'Facts' in a peremptory manner like a stage brigand calling for 'Wine!.'... In these letters I shall stick to the hardest of hard facts and the coldest of cold reasons.

He considers the appalling conditions of men, women and children working in mines and mills, the production of luxuries for the few while millions were short of basic necessities, he paints a picture of what might be — his Merrie England.

114

In many ways Robert Blatchford's conception of Merrie England may seem naive because we think of transforming *our* world into his Merrie England, not *his* world. His was a very different world, although the seeds of our world had all been sown.

His world included the wealthy land, mill and mine owners, identifiable individuals, often living locally. The workers knew about them, they knew whether they went to church (invariably they did), they knew a great deal about their morals and their money. Life was much more about real people and who cared for whom and who exploited whom, rather than about remote international financiers and institutions.

His world, for the working class, meant large families, five or six children or more, number of bedrooms one or two. No baths, no electricity. Gas lighting in the towns, oil lamps in the country. Heating and cooking confined to the coal-fired kitchen stove. Hours of work fifty to eighty each week. No education beyond ten years old for most children. No unemployment pay, no pensions, no health service, no annual holidays. Survival if all went well, near starvation if not.

It did not seem to early Socialists like Robert Blatchford and my mother and father that *Merrie England* was an impossible dream.

Ignorance

I feel sure that the time will come when people will find it difficult to believe that a rich community such as ours, having such command over external nature, could have submitted to live such a mean, shabby, dirty life as we do!

This quotation from William Morris heads a chapter in

Merrie England. The key words are 'submitted to live.' The problem was the ignorance of the rich, and the ignorance of the poor. In the main, rich and poor alike accepted that this was the way it was, and would continue to be. Voices from the pulpit even claimed that this was the way it was meant to be.

Twenty-five years ago I was speaking at a housing conference. I said that the slums of Liverpool, Belfast and Glasgow were amongst the worst in Europe. A man came up to me afterwards; he told me that he was a Belfast Councillor and he said, 'I have never yet seen the slums of Belfast.' He promised me that he would visit them and do something about them. For the first time he was going to find out how the other half lived.

Towards the end of the last century a few brave men challenged the existing ways and fought for change. Some of them had been brought up in grinding poverty, some were rich men who cared enough to find out how the other half lived and were horrified at what they saw. These men, poor and rich, from the soap box, and some from the pulpit, prayed, 'Thy will be done on earth as it is in heaven', and they knew that this meant revolutionary change in men and institutions.

Robert Blatchford in *The Clarion* and *Merrie England* challenged the whole industrial system as it was operated in his day. To care for everyone, to release the potential of everyone, this would be morally right. This was *The Clarion* call. He would not accept that what was morally right would bring about economic disaster as his opponents claimed it would.

How the Poor Lived
Robert Blatchford quoted the Registrar General's

returns from 1881 to 1889:

> The annual death rate of children under one year old per
> 100,000:-
>   For three farming counties   9,717
>   For three manufacturing towns 21,803

In a family living under industrial working and housing
conditions, one child in five did not live to see its first
birthday. When you see those old photographs with most
of the women wearing black, this is why.

A brief extract from a report by a Doctor Russell
illustrated the housing conditions of the poor:

> of the inhabitants of Glasgow, 29 % live in dwellings of one
> room.... No less than 14 % of one-roomed dwellings and 27
> % of the two-roomed dwellings, contain lodgers   strange
> men and women, mixed up with husbands, and wives, and
> children, within the four walls of small rooms.... There are
> thousands of these dwellings which contain five, six, seven
> inmates, and hundreds are inhabited by from eight to
> thirteen. Of all the children who die in Glasgow before they
> complete their fifth year, 32 % die in houses of one room, and
> not 2 % in dwellings of five rooms and upwards.... From the
> beginning to rapid ending these children play short parts in
> a wretched tragedy....

Robert Blatchford condemned the economic system
that created these conditions. He quotes Lord Salisbury
speaking on factory conditions in the House of Lords in
1873:

> Well can I recollect, in the earlier periods of the factory
> movement, waiting at the factory gates to see the children
> come out, and a set of sad, dejected, cadaverous creatures
> they were. In Bradford, especially, the people of long and
> cruel task were most remarkable. The cripples and distorted
> forms might be numbered by hundreds, perhaps by

thousands. A friend of mine collected a vast number together for me; the sight was most piteous, the deformities incredible.

He urges John Smith to read of these horrors in the Government Blue Books and the reports of the Labour Commission, to read the facts relating to the Truck Acts and the chain and nail trades:

> I grant you that Socialism would imply some interference with the liberty of the individual. But which individual? Imagine a dozen men at sea in a boat with only two days provisions. Would it be wise to consider the liberty of the individual? If the strongest man took all the food and left the others to starve would it be right or wrong for the eleven men to combine to bind him and divide all fairly?

There were employers who saw factory workers and their families as they saw the black slaves, as an inferior species unfit for anything better. Others were deeply concerned but felt that they were trapped by the competitive system. Better pay and conditions would mean higher prices and bankruptcy.

If these compassionate employers were right then surely Blatchford was right too, right to condemn the system under which they operated.

Food

Employers and Government justified the conditions in the mills on the basis that we needed to export manufactured goods in order to pay for imported corn to feed our growing population. Blatchford asked, 'is that really so or is it because men who are making rich profits cannot or will not see the truth? We have ample fertile land and unemployed men, why not grow our own corn?' He advanced two main reasons why this should be done:

To make it possible to abolish the slavery of the factory
system.
To avoid being starved into defeat if we should find ourselves
at war.

He quotes in some detail a number of authorities who
claimed we could feed two or three times the population
using traditional farming methods current at that time.
Not content with this he refers to the increased crop yields
achieved on a large scale under glass in Guernsey,
increased production by using better strains of wheat and
more scientific methods generally. He considers the
possibility of developing fishing and 'great fish-breeding
lakes.' He was concerned about the pollution of the
atmosphere from burning coal and recommends the
developing of other sources such as tide power, that even
one hundred years ago had been the subject of scientific
reports with particular reference to the tides at Bristol
and the Severn estuary.

Blatchford advanced these proposals not on a basis of
some economic or political theory, but because of his
passionate concern for the quality of life of the people.
He wanted everyone to have the necessities of life, that
for him meant not only food, clothing and housing, but
work, art, music, literature and an understanding of
nature. He carried in his mind the picture of the pale,
sickly children of the slums and factories. He had a vision
of these same children singing, dancing, playing in the
sunshine with roses in their cheeks.

In 1885 we exported cotton goods to the value of
£66,000,000, while we imported corn and flour to the
value of £53,000,000.

Robert Blatchford viewed these figures with alarm. The factory conditions that sustained these exports were inhuman in peace time and could bring unemployment and starvation in war time.

Robert Blatchford had served six years in the army and travelled extensively on the continent; the possibility of Britain becoming involved in war was much on his mind.

His view was that all the talk of our 'tight little island' and the 'Glories of the Empire' would be nonsense if we could not feed ourselves.

The pride of the British people was its manufacturing industry, the strength of the army and navy and the size and power of the Empire. Few had any doubt that the British Empire was inviolate and would last a thousand years.

Blatchford challenged these assumptions because he challenged the whole conception of a society based on materialistic values.

It would not be many years before another voice was to challenge British supremacy and our power to feed ourselves. 1914 was only twenty years away.

Waste

Blatchford was concerned that creative ability was wasted, and that a poor man had little chance, however gifted, to get the education and opportunity to develop. Blatchford himself only became a writer by a series of accidents when he was already thirty-four years old.

He writes of a few who emerged in spite of the system:

> William Smith, the greatest English geologist, he was a poor farmer's son and chiefly self taught: Sir William Herschel, the great astronomer, he played the oboe in a watering-place

band: there was Faraday a bookbinder, and Sir Humphrey Davy an apothecary's apprentice, both became great scientists: there was James Watt the mathematical instrument maker, and George Stephenson the collier, and Arkwright the barber, and Jacquard the weaver, and John Hunter the great anatomist who was a poor Scotch carpenter.

But how many more submerged in our uncaring society might have made great contributions to the welfare of our society:

The common people are like an untilled, unwatered, and unweeded garden. No one has yet studied or valued the capacities of men. It is not only the wrong of this I resent, it is the WASTE

Then he writes:

It makes me angry when I think of it, and I must be calm and practical, because you, John Smith, are such a shrewd hard-headed man – God help you.

Land

It was a fundamental belief among the old Socialists that the land was a common heritage of all people and that it was wrong that it should be appropriated by a few people to make money for themselves. Robert Blatchford gives an example of a duke who owns a large estate:

The estate is let out to farmers who pay the duke £30,000 a year in rent. Where do the farmers get this money from? The farmers sell their crops, and out of the purchase money pay the rent.... The rent is earned by the farmers and their men... not by the duke. The duke did not make the land, nor does he raise the crops. He has therefore no right to take the rent at all.

The man who gets rich on ground rent gets rich on the labour of others.

He tells the story of a nobleman who stops a tramp, who is crossing his park, and orders him off his land! The tramp asks him how the land came to be his. The noble replies that he inherited it from his father. 'How did he get it?', asks the tramp. 'From his father' is the reply. 'And how did your great, great, great etc. grandfather get it?', asks the tramp. The nobleman draws himself up, and replies, 'He fought for it and won it.' 'Then' says the unabashed vagrant, beginning to take off his coat, 'I will fight *you* for it!'

We see in these days land jumping in value by millions of pounds an acre as the result of the removal of planning restrictions. Faced with a similar situation in his day Robert Blatchford put the issue to John Smith that wealth is created by applying mind and muscle to the creation of necessary things; this is the wealth of the nation.

Men women and children were paying a heavy price in ill health and premature death to create wealth, while at the same time their real creative potential was wasted.

Should they not have better conditions and a fair share of the wealth they create?

Is it not wrong that a great proportion of that wealth should go in profit and rent to those that do not produce it?

Environment

Robert Blatchford was concerned about the ugly, unhealthy, inhuman environment in our industrial towns and cities — not only the bad housing but the lack of facilities for communal activities, education and recreation. We consider the best methods of feeding and caring for cattle and crops. We do this for all living things except man.

Robert Blatchford wanted to see everyone involved in doing what needs to be done – working together with one objective to create *Merrie England*.

So Robert Blatchford's challenge was: Think, think, think, if you like, dream. For 'where there is no vision the people perish.' He sketched out in very general terms what he would like to see built. It was community planning based on meeting everyone's needs. His dream looked very like Letchworth and Welwyn Garden City built a generation later.

Work

As Blatchford saw it, among those fit to work there were three sectors:

1. Idle rich. Producing nothing.
2. Workers producing non-necessities for the rich.
3. Workers producing necessities for themselves and groups 1 and 2.

He wanted to expand the third sector at the expense of the others for two reasons.

First, the third group having to produce necessities for the other two groups as well as themselves had to work excessive hours under appalling conditions. The greater the proportion of workers producing necessities, the shorter hours and better conditions they could enjoy.

Why should a farm worker have to work sixteen hours a day in order to feed the idle rich and producers of useless goods?

His second reason was interesting. Producing demonstrably useful commodities under good conditions was a satisfying way to live. Why not have more people involved in it? Class divisions would disappear and there would be enough and more than enough for all.

Blatchford was at considerable pains to convince working class people that they should not envy the rich their way of life, or the middle class theirs. He had the temerity to lambast English cooking and ridicule fashionable clothes and the clutter of the Victorian drawing room. He wanted John Smiths to look with fresh eyes at our whole way of life. Live simply: keep the good and throw out all that was unworthy.

He thought the whole idea of competition was ludicrous. The idea of setting one company against another, devising means of defeating the other, like two boxers in the ring striving to win on points or on a knock-out if they could. What sort of civilisation was that?

> It was evil in its origin, in its progress, in its methods, in its motives, and in its effects. No nation can be sound whose motive power is greed.

The British people could produce a great deal more of the good things of life than the narrow thinking of the materialist allowed, more than enough for everyone. If he could convince everyone of this then we were on our way.

If one takes too much, somewhere someone will have too little. There could be more than enough, and in his delightful phrase 'enough is *better* than a feast.'

MERRIE ENGLAND

BY

ROBERT BLATCHFORD

(NUNQUAM.)

DEDICATED TO

A. M. THOMPSON

(DANGLE.)

PRICE ONE PENNY.

1894.
LONDON:
Clarion Office, 4, Bouverie Street, Fleet Street, E.C.; WALTER SCOTT,
24, Warwick Lane, E.C.

Priorities

This was Robert Blatchford's Socialism. It was not about the class war or workers' control or the ideology of Karl Marx. It was about creating resources, using resources, about meeting the needs of people. *About priorities.*

He believed that most middle and upper class people did not even know about the deprivation suffered by the poor and that most working class people did not understand that the resources were available to meet their needs.

He believed that our nation was well capable of providing the basic necessities and more for every man, woman and child in the land.

It seemed to him that democracy should elect a Government to do just that.

Why not?

Week by week in *The Clarion* he battled to explain what to him was obvious. He would quote Greek philosophers, set out the argument step by step like a mathematical equation, put it into a modern parable or a comic story. Often he must have felt that he was banging his head against a brick wall of indifference. But he never gave up; he never would give up while children died of preventable diseases, men's talents were wasted, babies died in their mothers' arms because there was no food, and old people were buried in paupers' graves.

So he spells it out:

> All things made by man may be divided into two classes, necessities and luxuries. I should include under necessities food, clothing, fuel, musical instruments and books.
>
> Now, it is evident that all these things, whether luxuries or necessities are made by labour. Diamond rings, loaves of

bread, grand pianos, and flat irons, do not grow on trees. They must be made by the labour of people, and it is very clear that the more luxuries a people produce the fewer necessities they will produce.

If a community consists of ten thousand people, and if nine thousand are making bread and one thousand are making jewellery, it is evident that there will be more bread than jewellery.

If in the same community nine thousand make jewellery and one thousand are making bread, there will be more jewellery than bread.

In the first case there will be food enough for all, though jewels be scarce. In the second case the people must starve, although they wear diamond rings on all their fingers.

In a well ordered state no luxuries would be produced until there were enough necessities for all.

There are now in this country an immense number of paupers, beggars and criminals as well as a large army of unemployed.... All these are supported by the workers, as is an idle rich peer with a rent roll of half a million a year. This is not only a waste of wealth and a waste of power, it is also a most wicked and disgraceful waste of human souls!

Paid Agitators

The speakers who came down our way when I was a boy often stayed in our home. We lived on three floors above my father's little shop and we had five bedrooms. So they came, MPs and miners, temperance speakers and trade unionists. A young clergyman from Poplar stayed once, when he sat down in front of the fire he threw back his long cassock to display breeches, thick stockings and hobnailed boots. His total possessions for a speaking tour he carried in a small haversack. This is how Jesus sent his men out all those years ago, and this is how many of the Socialist speakers went out, not knowing where they would find a meal or a bed.

In the 1920s I remember seven Welsh miners sitting round our big kitchen table. They were part of a choir touring the country to raise money for the strike fund. My mother was one of a family of nine children, my father of eight, so my two brothers and I, plus the extra seven was just like the old days. She loved it. I was with my mother when she took them to their rooms; for one of them she had a small fold-up 'camp' bed. He was a substantially built man. Mother said at once 'I am sorry. You can't sleep on that. I'll find you another bed.' He said 'Mrs. Moncrieff, if that is the bed you have for me, that is where I will sleep.' Knowing my mother I had not expected the large miner to win the argument, but he did. I was expecting to lose my room and be relegated to the top staircase landing in that bed. Not for the first time.

No fair-minded man who took the trouble to get to know these men would call them 'paid agitators.' They sacrificed for what they believed. No man can do more.

Robert Blatchford was very rarely to be found on a public platform; his job was to pass the ammunition, but he was incensed that in a free country men could be hounded because of what they believed. So he wrote:

> The capitalist press... are in the habit of abusing Socialists. Socialist speakers are commonly described as 'Paid Agitators.'.. battening on the earnings of ignorant dupes. 'When a paper calls a man a 'paid agitator' it implies that he is a liar and a rogue, who is preaching what he knows to be false and preaching it for the sake of making money.... This is a lie.

Take John Burns. He is an engineer. Being a good workman he could earn two pounds a week and not work more that fifty-five hours. I can remember an appeal for subscriptions to raise his income of one pound a week, paid by the Dockers union, to two pounds.... His working hours are all the hours he can spare from sleep. The first time I saw him was during the Glasgow strike. He had made five long speeches that day. He was so hoarse that I could hardly hear him speak. He looked utterly fagged out, and that night he went to a cheap Temperance Hotel and had weak tea and bread and butter for his supper.

It is difficult in these days of microphones to realise the sheer physical effort of doing five outdoor meetings in an evening, often in the open air.

My father did this often at election times. He would come home physically exhausted, his throat was raw and used to haemorrhage. He once spoke at an open air meeting in the square at Dover. The crowd was so large it stopped the traffic. I think it was at this meeting where a voice from the crowd demanded to know what he was, assuming him to be a 'paid agitator.' He calmly and truthfully replied 'I am a pigeon fancier by inclination, a tailor by accident, and a Socialist by conviction.'

George Lansbury travelled the length and breadth of the country. He recalled:

.... It was my custom, directly my work was finished on Saturday, to leave London for the provinces, do a meeting on Saturday night, three on Sunday, and catch the train back, ready to start work at seven o'clock on Monday morning. My trains would land me at the London terminus at all hours - 3.00, 3.30, 4, 5 o'clock in the morning, often it was my lot to walk to Bow from Kings Cross and Euston. Always when arriving home at these early hours my wife would be waiting up with a first class breakfast....

George Lansbury's beloved Bessie was typical of the wonderful wives who backed these men. Some of them, of course, like my mother were not unfamiliar with the platform in their own right.

No wonder Robert Blatchford spoke with anger at the newspaper jibes of 'paid agitator.' He knew John Burns exhausted after five long speeches, George Lansbury huddled in a freezing train through the night, my father spitting blood.

The Church

Robert Blatchford challenged the Church to teach and church-goers to live what Jesus taught. Fair enough; but there was a bitterness in the way he attacked the Church that was out of keeping with the normal behaviour of this warm compassionate man. Why? We shall never know now, but there must have been something in his own life to which he needed an answer, but that none of his Christian friends helped him find. He criticised the Church because it failed society; he did it with bitterness because it failed him. He did not seem to have had a Christian to challenge and care for him as Ben Tillett had in Cardinal Manning, as Will Crooks had in the Rev. John Wilson.

For his criticism of the Church in its failure to meet the needs and aspirations of the common people there was support to be had from within the Church. He himself quoted Bishop Gore of Birmingham who wrote in his pamphlet, 'The Social Doctrine of the Sermon on the Mount':

> Bad dwellings, inadequate wages, inadequate education, inability to use leisure – these are stones that lie upon graves

of the spiritually dead. We must take away those stones.

He quotes Shaftesbury who wrote, at the time of the agitation for the Ten Hours Bill for women and children in factories:

> I find, as usual, the clergy are in many cases frigid, in some hostile. So it has ever been with me. At first I could get none, at last I have obtained a few, but how miserable a proposition of the whole class!.... They are timid time serving, and great worshippers of wealth and power. I can scarcely remember an instance in which a clergyman has been found to maintain the cause of labourers in the face of pew holders.

The outspoken words of men such as these should have restrained him from attacking the Church as a whole. He offended many Socialist Christians to no purpose.

Blame and Punishment

Robert Blatchford was clear that everyone was born with their own special character, but there was within it vast potential for good or evil and talents that could be fostered or frustrated. The conditions each person was brought up in became a major factor in how they behaved and what they achieved, and so he writes:

> I claim that men should not be classed as good and bad but as fortunate and unfortunate; that they should be pitied, and not blamed, helped instead of being punished.

There was little support for this approach in those days. The Law and the Church believed that wrongdoing should be severely punished, involving years in prison, flogging and hanging in this life and hell fire in the life to come. A man who murdered his wife and a hungry child who stole a loaf of bread, in the eyes of Judge and Magistrate, were both evil and had to be punished for their sins and as a warning to others. This was wrong; if Society had denied a delinquent child a decent home and environment, then it was Society that should be condemned along with the Government, the Magistrate and the Bishop that upheld such monstrous injustice.

So Blatchford writes:

> .... They uphold blame and punishment, in defiance of the teaching and example of Jesus Christ. The founder of their religion bade them love their enemies. He taught them that if one stole their coat they should give him their cloak also. He prevented the punishment of the woman taken in adultery, and called upon him without sin to cast the first stone. He asked God to forgive his murderers, because they knew not what they did. In not one of these cases did Christ say a word in favour of punishment nor of blame.

> It is with moral evils as with physical evils. When an epidemic of fever or smallpox comes upon us we do not punish the sick, nor blame them. But we isolate the sick, and we attack the *cause* of the sickness, by attending to matters of hygiene and sanitation. That is how we ought to deal with moral sickness.

We have Begun

Robert Blatchford writes:

> Socialism will not come by means of a sudden coup. It will... develop naturally and by degrees. It always amuses me to hear the intensely practical person demand, 'How are you going to do it? When will you start?'

> My dear Mr. Smith, it is too late to ask where we are going to begin. We *have* begun. Nearly all law is more or less Socialistic, for nearly all law implies the right of the State to control individuals for the benefit of the nation.... The

abolition of toll bars and bridge tolls was Socialistic action, for it made the roads and bridges common property.

Most of the Building Acts, by virtue of which streets must be a specified width, back-to-back houses are forbidden etc, are Socialistic, for they take away from the property owners the power to do as he likes with his own.

The Factory Acts are Socialistic, for they deny the employer the power to work women and children to death.

The Compulsory and Free Education Acts are Socialistic. The Acts which compel the inspection of mines and factories, inspection of boilers, the placing of a load line on ships, and the granting of relief to paupers, are all Socialistic Acts, for they all interfere with the 'freedom of contract', and the 'rights of the individual.'

Finally the acquirement of the postal and telegraphic arrangements by the State, and the establishment of corporate gas and water works are Socialistic measures, for they recognise the Socialist principle of common ownership, production and distribution. You will see then, that Socialism has begun, so that the question of where to begin is quite superfluous.

What Now?

We want to find work for the unemployed. We want to get pensions for the aged. We want to abolish the poor-law system. We want to produce our own food so as to be independent of foreign nations. We want to get rid of slums and build good houses for the workers. We want to abolish the sweater and shorten hours and raise wages. We want to get rid of the smoke nuisance, and the pollution of rivers; and we want to place the land and all instruments of production under the control of the State.

Perhaps we should begin with the land. Perhaps with the unemployed. Perhaps with the mines and railways.

Many Liberals, academics, philanthropists and churchmen, who were by no means socialists, had also come to the conclusion that communal enterprise as opposed to private enterprise was necessary to meet many of the needs of the day. Liberals had already been responsible for much that had been done and in many large towns and cities elaborate headquarters were built for their municipal gas and water undertakings and many still stand as their monuments today. The question for Socialists was whether more progress could be made in these future objectives with the Liberals in office. Socialists found Liberals opposing some of these issues and paying only lip service to others as implementation cut across the self-interest of those of them who were land and factory owners. Communal activity was one thing, dismantling capitalism was another; the first was socialistic, the second was Socialism.

Robert Blatchford felt that in this situation the leaders of the working class should be concentrating on winning people one by one to an understanding of the moral basis for socialism and the personal challenge to each one to apply the philosophy to their own lives. So he states, 'It is necessary not only to improve your conditions but improve yourselves.' So he quotes Jesus about 'loving your neighbour as yourself.' For him putting your faith in organisations from the Church of England to the Independent Labour Party was dangerous. So he belonged to none of them. It is a sobering and challenging thought. Too many people support good causes by a small subscription but not by giving themselves. Penny in the slot Socialism, or penny in the slot Christianity, you put in your penny and out comes a bar of chocolate, until one day you find that nobody has refilled the machine.

Robert Blatchford was a Socialist; he wrote:

> Socialism will come, of that I feel sure. It will come by paths not seen by me, and it will develop in ways I do not dream of, my task is to help its arrival.

Unlike Keir Hardie, Ben Tillett and the others he thought that education, training people to live the life, should come first, before creating organisations. It is difficult to understand why he should not accept, as they did, that both could develop together.

Robert Blatchford devoted his life to a joyous crusade to expose what was wrong, to make people think and to teach men to live what was right. To end the waste of wealth and the waste of lives. He did not organise activities. He inspired fellowship, he breathed warmth and love into people. His influence cannot be measured, but most of the one million copies sold of *Merrie England*, like the one I have with its tattered pages and cover held together with sticky tape, passed through many hands.

The weekly *Clarion* continued publication until 1935 and Robert Blatchford died in 1943 at the age of ninety two.

When my father died at the age of only fifty-two in 1930 my brother John and my mother asked Robert Blatchford to write a few words to go on his tombstone. His simple words are as apt for Robert Blatchford himself as they were for his old friend:

> Let us do all the good we can,
> Try to be happy here,
> Try to make others happy,
> And when the veil is lifted
> We shall see.

Robert Blatchford in the last pages of *Merrie England* described the England of his day and put the challenge to 'John Smith', to the millions of men and women who would read his words:

> Go out into the streets of any big English town and use your eyes, John. What do you find? You find some rich and idle, wasting unearned wealth to their own shame and injury, and the shame and injury of others. You find hard working people packed away in vile unhealthy streets. You find little children famished, dirty and half naked outside the luxurious clubs, shops, hotels, and theatres. You find men and women overworked and underpaid. You find vice and want and disease cheek by jowl with religion culture and wealth. You find the usurer, the gambler, the fop, the finnikin fine lady, and you find the starveling, the slave, the vagrant, the drunkard, and the harlot.
>
> Do your duty, John. Do not lie to your soul any more. Long have you known that injustice and misery are rife amongst the people, If you have not acted upon the knowledge it is not because you knew it to be useless so to act, but because you were lazy and preferred your ease, or because you were selfish and feared to lose your own advantage, or because you were heartless and did not really feel any pang at the sight of the sufferings of others.
>
> I say that wrong and sorrow are here crushing the life out of our brothers and sisters. I say that you in common with all men, are responsible for the things that are. I say that it is your duty to seek the remedy; and I say that if you seek it you will find it.

So Robert Blatchford taught men and women the realities of the under privileged in the society of his day. He created socialists; not socialism that was for the future; but socialists which for him meant men and women who cared and shared and built a joyous fellowship across the land.

Not so idle rich

Frances, Countess of Warwick, published this story in her reminiscences, she called it the 'curious strange adventure' that happened to her in 1895. It changed her life:

There had been a grand ball at the Castle. Of course the ball was a great success, and the newspapers applauded with great enthusiasm, all except one obscure sheet, *The Clarion*. This paper only reached me on the second morning after the ball; and my attention was called to its special article about the ball by an ominous black line. I read with indignation and amazement a violent attack on myself for holding idle junketing in a time of general misery. This 'impertinent rag' said scathingly that ours was a sham benevolence, a frivolous ignoring of real social conditions. I was so angry that the memory of that anger is vivid still. I said to myself that the writer of this article was some crabbed, envious being, who begrudged the chance of work to the poor people who had their share of the money spent on the festivities; someone who hated luxury because it was out of his reach.

In my bitter indignation, I forgot all about my duty to my guests who still lingered. I got up at once, told my maid that I was going to London by the earliest train, and leaving the Castle without a word of explanation to anyone, I was in Fleet Street by midday searching for the editorial office of *The Clarion*. I found this office at the top of a staircase in one of the older buildings of the street, with the editor's name, Robert Blatchford, on the door. I entered unannounced, and there at his writing desk sat the man who had dared to attack us for indulging in legitimate amusement that had at the same time given honest work to so many unemployed.

His coldly gazing eyes showed no surprise at the unexpected and abrupt vision in his dingy office of a young woman dressed in the height of fashion. He made no movement of welcome. I remembered thinking that the garment he wore, which was something between a dressing gown and a lounge coat, was most undignified. 'Are you the editor of *The Clarion*?', I demanded. He merely nodded. 'I came about this', I went on, thrusting the marked page under his eyes. He made no reply but his preoccupied eye seemed to hold a question and he waited for me to go on. 'How could you be so unfair, so unjust?', I asked. 'Our ball has given work to half the county, and to dozens of dressmakers in London besides.'

'Will you sit down', he replied, 'while I explain to you how mistaken you are about the real effect of luxury' And then Robert Blatchford told me, as a Socialist and a Democrat, what he thought of charity bazaars and ladies bountiful. He made it plain to me the difference between productive and unproductive labour. He said that labour used to produce finery was as much wasted as if it were used to dig holes in the ground and fill them in again.

By this new standard I found nine tenths of the money spent on the Warwick Ball had been wasted. Such elementary economics as that the only useful labour was labour that produced useful articles, which in turn helped labour to produce again, was all new to me. Although I had a vague idea that money spent on champagne and delicacies was wasted, I found that the Blatchford doctrine included the cobwebby lace and similar useless and beautiful things in the same category.

My old ideas and ideals were brought to naught, and it was late in the afternoon before this plain man with the big ideas had ceased speaking. We had both forgotten the lunch hour and the passing of time.

Of course I did not grasp all that was poured into my hungry soul, but before the end of the talk I did realize humbly that setting the poor, who themselves needed food and coal and decent housing, to build unnecessary rooms for an evening's enjoyment, to cook dainties for people already overfed, and to make clothes for the rich dancers, was idle work. The great ball, and all its preparations, I found had not added one iota to the national wealth.

I was somewhat dazed when I at last left Fleet Street and got to the railway station, where I sat waiting for the train to take me back to Warwick. During the journey home I thought and thought about all that I had been hearing and learning. I knew my outlook on life could never be the same as before the incident. I reached home just as my wondering guests were going into dinner, and when I joined the party I made no effort to satisfy the curiosity and explain my odd absence. I was as one who had found a new, a real world. The crisis I was facing, or had faced, was emotional, and it would have been impossible then to frame such an experience in words. Indeed, it took much hard intellectual effort during several years before I could be said to have intelligently grasped and become persuaded that Socialism was the only solution to the problem of poverty. I was, however, an apt and ardent pupil. Next day I sent for ten pounds worth of books on Socialism. I got the name of an old Professor of Economics, and under him I started my period of study without delay. It would be idle to try to follow the circuitous path I trod, but it was Robert Blatchford's honest talk on the memorable day that gave me a vision of how it would be possible to change and modify the unjust conditions of our modern life.

Eleven years later the 'curious strange adventure' of

the Countess of Warwick was still continuing, as in her red motor car she supported Will Thorne during his successful campaign to win West Ham for Labour in the famous election of 1906.

Out of the Pit

Keir was born in Lanarkshire to his unmarried mother Mary Keir on 15 August 1856. She had to bring him up alone for the first three years of his life. His natural father refused to recognise him. Later Mary married David Hardie; by him she had six children. David Hardie worked at whatever job he could get, carpenter, miner, seaman. The family had good times and bad; good, was when you got a whole egg for breakfast on Sunday, bad, was when everything in the house that was saleable had been sold and there was no food in the house.

It was right that Keir Hardie throughout his life carried the name Keir; Mary never gave up. Above all she taught him to read and write and fostered his passion for books and words. He had had only a few months schooling when he became one of the family bread-winners at seven years old.

At one time when things were bad at home, Mary was expecting a baby and one of the children was ill and near death. Keir was working as a baker's errand boy; his four shillings and sixpence a week was the only family income. David Hardie at that time was a victim of a lockout of Clyde shipworkers. Keir recalled in later years an incident that he described as 'not only a turning-point in my life, but also in my outlook upon men and things....':

One winter's morning I turned up at the baker's shop where I was employed and was told I had to go upstairs to see the master. I was kept waiting outside the door of the dining room while he said grace – he was noted for religious zeal – and, on being admitted, found the master and his family seated round a large table. He was serving out bacon and eggs while his wife was pouring coffee.... I had never seen such a beautiful room, nor such a table, loaded as it was with food and beautiful things. The master read me a lecture before the assembled family on the sin of slothfulness, and added that though he would forgive me for that once, if I sinned again by being late I would be instantly dismissed.

Keir was given no chance to explain that he had had no breakfast and had been up most of the night tending his sick brother and helping his mother:

Two mornings afterwards I was again a few minutes late, for the same cause and was informed on arriving at the shop that I was discharged and my fortnight's wages forfeited by way of punishment.

That night the baby was born. The next morning, 1 January 1867, there was no fire or food in the house. His sick brother died.

The fact that the baker and his family were well fed was the product of night baking, delivery on time, and employing cheap labour. That was the system, that's how it was. But the baker was a Churchman. To go to Church say your prayers and not 'love your delivery boy as yourself' was a travesty of what Jesus taught. Many workers who understood full well what Jesus taught turned from the Church because of this hypocrisy. Some in bitterness and disbelief. Some to find their own way with the help of the Bible and the knowledge that Jesus and many of his friends were workers like them.

Mary and David Hardie began to question the conventional Christianity they had taught their children after these bitter experiences. On the same shelf as the *Bible* and *The Pilgrim's Progress* were Paine's *Age of Reason*, Wilson's *Tales of the Borders*, and the poems of Robert Burns.

Keir, ten years old now, went down the pit as a 'trapper'; his job for six and a half days a week was to sit alone opening and shutting a ventilation door. Later he became a pony driver. Besides working down the pit he attended Fraser's night school at Holytown. There was no light provided by the school; the pupils had to bring their own candles. Primitive though it was, he was learning and he began to read widely encouraged by Mary.

David Hardie found work on the railway being built between Edinburgh and Glasgow and life at home was better. There was a fire in the grate in the winter and by its side Mary recited ballads and folk tales.

Into the Community

Keir Hardie, by the time he was twenty, was an experienced miner and he had added shorthand to his reading and writing. He took part in the temperance movement speaking at meetings indoors and out. He was becoming a master of the written and the spoken word.

However his experiences in childhood and in the pits had made him a bitter and cynical young man. If this attitude had continued he might well have used his developing capacity for leadership to rouse men to bitter confrontation and violence.

Something happened at this time that was to alter Keir's whole life and outlook. One day he wrote in his diary, 'Today I have given my life to Jesus Christ.' He did not explain or elaborate, but the effect was profound. His bitterness disappeared and compassion filled his spirit for the sufferings of all men, women and children everywhere. With this compassion came a determination to build a just and equal society on the basis of the Sermon on the Mount. Throughout the rest of his life he rode all the injustices, the attacks and dirty tricks and set out to make his enemies into friends and his friends into fighters for a new world.

Thirty-six years later Keir said, 'The impetus which drove me first of all into the Labour Movement and the inspiration which has carried me on in it, has been derived more from the teachings of Jesus of Nazareth than all the other sources combined.'

Keir was not only active in the community, his brother miners made him their spokesman in taking grievances to the management. The owners soon had enough of this, and he along with his two younger brothers was sacked with the parting words, 'We'll hae nae damned Hardies in this pit.'

The mineowners had declared war on him and he accepted the challenge. They had declared war on the men too. In this time of depression wages were reduced to two shillings a day in the district where Hardie had worked and down to one shilling and eightpence elsewhere. Keir, banned from the mines, became a correspondent to the *Glasgow Weekly Mail*, but he continued his work for the miners.

At the age of twenty-three Keir was becoming a major speaker at miners' meetings, and on 3 July 1879 he was appointed Corresponding Secretary of the Lanarkshire miners. In August of that year at a mass meeting he was voted the miners' Agent by a large majority in October at the National Conference he was appointed National Secretary.

Good fellowship was a natural part of all the workers' activities of the day, the Free Churches, the Cooperative Movement, the Temperance Movement and the Trade Unions. This meant a great deal to Keir who could recite Burns, sing a song and make merry with the best of them. Good fellowship and caring created these movements and the movements created good fellowship and caring. In the Temperance Movement Keir met Lillie Wilson, daughter of a miner; they married in 1880 and moved to Ayrshire where Keir had been asked to use his Lanarkshire experience and organise the miners.

Miners' March

After a year of quiet persuasion laced with powerful oratory, Keir had reached the whole of his new Ayrshire territory. There was still little organisation as we would understand it today, but there was a closer fellowship, a stirring of the spirit. In August 1881 a claim for a ten percent rise in wages was submitted and rejected.

At two o'clock the next Monday morning the Annbank brass band came playing through Trabboch village and miners jumped out of bed and fell in behind. Away up towards Auchinleck they went marching, their numbers increasing with every mile of road. On through Darnconner and Cronberry and Lugar and Muirkirk, right on to Glenbuck then down to Cumnock, now at least five thousand strong. Other bands were marching from colliery to colliery and all the roads round about Galston village and Hurlford and Crookedholm and Riccarton were filled with the colliers marching towards Craigie Hill. To what extent this was planned and to what extent it was spontaneous was never satisfactorily explained.

The fact is that in one day an almost complete stoppage of the Ayrshire mining industry had been achieved by the bands and the marching men.

The strike lasted ten weeks. The bands went collecting money, farmers gave meal and potatoes to keep the children from starving and men, women and children earned a few shillings here and there at harvesting and odd jobs.

In the end the remarkable fine autumn weather turned cold, all resources were gone and the men marched back to work. They had not got their rise in wages but they were now a force to be reckoned with. Within a month, with an upturn in trade, the owners increased wages without being asked, an action without precedent.

Keir maintained himself and his family somewhat precariously in those days with a little writing for newspapers. Then the pastor of the local Evangelical Church that Keir had joined was in bad health and asked Keir to take over from him the writing of the local notes for the *Cumnock News*. Keir was soon acting as editor. The paper was an offshoot of the *Ardrossan and Saltcoats Herald*; the owner and editor was Arthur Guthrie, a staunch Liberal, who had the courage to stand up to the Tory mine and land-owning families who dominated the county.

Keir's astonishing capacity for work was used in those days in many causes. In addition to his steady work with the miners and newspaper work, he held the chief office in the local Good Templars. He preached the gospel of Jesus at street corners and occasionally in the pulpit. He taught at local evening classes and read extensively Carlyle, Emerson and Ruskin and his beloved Robert

Burns.

In August 1886 the Ayrshire Miners Union was formed, Andrew Fisher, later Prime Minister of Australia, was one of the earliest delegates. Hardie as Organising Secretary had a salary of £75 a year and was also appointed Secretary to the Scottish Miners Federation that was formed the same year.

Working men had been looking to the Liberal Party in Parliament to secure them the vote and progress was made in the Reform Act of 1884. The Liberal Party in some areas welcomed working men candidates; two miners had been elected to Parliament in 1874 under the Liberal banner. The question of whether working men could trust the Liberal Party to support their interests or whether they had to go it alone was under discussion throughout the land.

Path to Parliament

In 1887 Keir Hardie was adopted as the miners' parliamentary candidate for North Ayrshire. Speaking at Irvine in October of that year he said:

> The Liberals and Conservatives have, through their organisations, selected candidates. They are both, as far as I know, good men. The point is these men have been selected without the mass of people being consulted. We are told that Sir William Wedderburn is a good Radical, and that he is sound on the Liberal programme, it may all be true, but we do not know whether it is or not. Will he, for example, support an Eight hour Bill? Nobody has asked him, and nobody cares except ourselves. Is he prepared to establish a wage court that would secure to the workman a just reward for his labour? Nobody knows whether he is or not. Is he prepared to support the extension of the Employers Liability Act, which presently limits compensation for loss of life, however culpable the

employer may be, to three years wage? Nobody knows. I am not surprised at the action of the Liberal association in opposing me....

Keir Hardie's view at that time was to put the Liberals and Radicals on trial. What precisely would they offer in return for working class support?

Keir Hardie's attitude grew out of his pride in the working class. This gave him integrity, he walked tall in any company and could not be patronised. If a man could say I am a miner or a seaman or a carpenter that was as much honour as any man could claim. In later years George Bernard Shaw recognised that Keir Hardie was the embodiment of 'the dignity of man' and described him as 'the damndest natural aristocrat in the House of Commons.'

In the same year, 1887, he launched *The Miner* where he wrote about many issues besides the problems of the mining industry. He considers the need for change and where it must start and he writes, '...the moment the masses come to feel and act as if they were men, that moment inequality ceases.' Nor did he see any reason to hide the source of his faith:

> The world today is sick and weary at heart. Even our clergy are to the most part dumb dogs who dare not bark. So it was in the days of Christ. They who proclaimed a God-given Gospel to the world were the poor and comparatively unlettered. We need a return to the principles of that Gospel, which, by proclaiming all men as sons of God and brethren one with another, makes it impossible for one, Shylock-like, to insist on his rights at the expense of another.

His day-to-day work was staggering. He writes in his first Annual Report to the Scottish Miners Federation

'.... I find, leaving out the deputations to London and the big conferences, that I have attended on behalf of the federation 77 meetings, 37 of which have been public, and 40 executive and Conference meetings, involving 6,000 miles of railway travel. I have sent out 1500 letters and circulars, and over 60,000 printed leaflets.' His work as secretary of the Ayrshire Miners was, of course, in addition to work for the Federation and various other organisations, such as a visit to London to see the Home Secretary about amendments to the Government's Miners Bill. Comfortable parliamentarians were faced with Keir Hardie in the Lobby, a man who had worked a regular twelve hours a day underground at ten years old. An amendment to the Bill to restrict boys' work underground to eight hours a day was defeated. An Amendment to prohibit boys under twelve years old working underground was carried. Westminster had not seen the last of the man from the pit. Perhaps this occasion marked the beginning of the end of hopes that the Liberals would at the end of the day back the workers and their wives and children.

There was a colliery disaster at Udston, in Lanarkshire, on 18 May 1887 and eighty-five lives were lost, many of them old friends of Keir. He hurried across from Ayrshire and took part in the relief work and did what he could to comfort the families of those lost. Keir Hardie put the blame squarely on the mineowners for being unwilling to provide adequate safety measures and on the Government inspectorate for gross neglect.

In the spring of 1888 Mr. Stephen Mason, Member of Parliament for Mid-Lanark, resigned and a by-election was called. Would the Liberal Party select a Scottish working class candidate. If so the mining community was putting forward Keir Hardie. His policy would be mainly that of a radical liberal plus a number of other proposals particularly with regard to the mining industry. In his election address he said, 'I adopt in its entirety the Liberal Programme... which includes Adult Suffrage; Reform of Registration Laws; Allotments for Labourers; County Government; London Municipal Government; Free Education; Disestablishment.' Many Liberals would support all this on election day but they were not always so forthcoming in Parliament. For the mines he would advocate 'An eight hour day for miners, and Insurance and Superannuation Funds.... Arbitration Courts and the creation of a Ministry of Mines....'

The Liberals offered Keir Hardie a seat in Parliament and £300 a year at the next General Election if he would withdraw on this occasion in favour of a young lawyer Mr. J.W. Phillips. Keir proposed that the local Liberals should choose their own candidate, but this proposal was rejected and Keir stood as an independent labour candidate.

The result was	Liberal	3847
	Conservative	2917
	Independent Labour	617

The Liberals and Conservatives had the full backing in organisation and finance of their national organisations. Keir had little finance, a scratch organisation, and was the subject of misrepresentation and abuse in the press. We shall never know what would have happened if the local Liberals had been given the chance to choose their own candidate as Keir Hardie advocated.

The result caused not despair but a determination to

break with the Liberals. On 25 August 1888 a Conference was held in the Waterloo Rooms, Glasgow and the Scottish Parliamentary Labour Party was formed. The officials were:

Hon. President	R.B. Cunninghame Graham.
Hon. Vice Presidents	Dr. G.B. Clark MP.
	and John Ferguson.
Chairman of the Executive	J. Shaw Maxwell.
Secretary	J. Keir Hardie.
Treasurer	George Mitchell.

This was not a socialist organisation, it was an organisation aiming to get working men into Parliament to advocate measures that would alleviate the suffering and improve the lot of the working people. Nevertheless some of these proposals were socialistic and would be unacceptable to the majority of Liberals.

Keir Hardie pursued this theme later in the same year at the annual Trade Union Congress held at Bradford, speaking in favour of Parliamentary Labour representation and the legal Eight Hour day. He was also at the Congress invited to preside over a meeting of overseas delegates from France, Holland, Belgium, Denmark and Italy. (Apparently some misunderstanding was responsible for the absence of the Germans.) Although the meeting was at the invitation of the TUC it brought together members of the Socialist International with Keir Hardie and other British trade unionists. Keir was greatly struck by the liveliness and determination of the visitors and enjoyed their company and recorded 'They are Socialists to a man and have the fiery zeal which always characterises earnest men who are fighting for a principle.... This may be a madness without method, ours is a method without life. A fusion of the two would be beneficial all round.' For the rest of his life he was active in the work of International Socialists.

Keir's proposal on the subject of free associations was put to the Conference and carried:

> The Labour parties in the different countries are requested to put on their programme, and work for, by agitation, the abolition of all laws prohibiting or hampering the free right of association and combination, national and international, of the workers.

Keir Hardie had entered the year 1888 as a Christian Radical prepared to stand as a working class Liberal candidate for Parliament. He ended it as an International Socialist with a dawning vision of the Brotherhood of Man under the Fatherhood of God. A vision that grew and deepened to the end of his days.

There were hundreds of local working class bodies at that time studying and discussing the shape of a new society and how it was to be achieved. Local electoral associations were now set up, but the 1884 Act also released a flood of hope and ideas throughout existing mainly working class organisations, Trade Unions, Cooperatives, the Temperance Movement, Working Men's Clubs and the Free Churches.

It is vital to understand that ALL THESE BODIES WERE ORGANISED AS ONE MAN ONE VOTE LOCALLY BASED DEMOCRACIES. Within them a vast number of working people had day to day experience of democracy, electing representatives, sitting on committees, formulating and moving resolutions, determining policy, public speaking. Few Conservatives had any such experience. Keir Hardie knew that there was an army out there already trained, so he continued to work within all these organisations. They contained the men and ideas that would take working men on to Local Councils and to Westminster. In these years he got through more work, spoke to more people in more places than almost any other man.

When a General Election was called in 1892 he was invited to stand not for a Scottish mining constituency but in London for West Ham. The local Liberals were in a dilemma, their chosen candidate had died and they decided not to bring in a new candidate at the last minute.

In his election address he said:

> I have all my life given independent support to the Liberal Party, but my first concern is the moral and material welfare of the working classes, and if returned, I will in every case place the claims of Labour above those of party. Generally speaking, I am in agreement with the present programme of the Liberal Party as far as it goes, but I reserve to myself the absolute and unconditional right to take such action, irrespective of the exigencies of party welfare as may to me seem needful in the interests of the workers.

At a conference of Trade Unions, Temperance Societies, other associations and clubs Keir was asked if he would follow Gladstone. He replied, 'So long as he was engaged in good democratic work, but if he opposed Labour questions he would oppose him or anybody else.' Asked if he would join the Liberal and Radical Party he replied, 'I expect to form an Independent Labour Party.'

Keir Hardie and the working class generally had supported the work of the Liberal governments under Gladstone. For example, the Ballot Act of 1872 had brought in the secret ballot, of immense importance to workers. Many of them knew that to vote openly for a candidate not supported by their employers would mean the sack. Then there was the 1880 Education Act that brought in compulsory schooling for five to ten year olds, too late for Keir Hardie's generation, but my father had benefited from it, staying at school until he was ten. This was indeed an advance although to be thrown onto the labour market at ten years old was no great prospect.

Some working class candidates, called Lib/Labs, were committed to the Liberal Party, others were prepared to accept Liberal support but without such commitment. These were the independent labour candidates.

Members of Parliament
In the 1892 General Election three independent labour candidates were elected:

> John Burns was elected at Battersea with 5616 votes to the Conservatives 4057.
> James Keir Hardie was elected at West Ham South with 5268 votes to the Conservatives 4036.
> James Havelock Wilson was elected at Middlesborough with 4691 votes to the Liberal 4062 and a Liberal Unionist 3333.

There were also eleven Lib/Labs elected; six were miners with four other trade unionists and one Radical who had supported Keir Hardie in Scotland, Dr. G.B. Clark. There were also two working class Irish candidates elected.

This might look as though there was a Labour group of three with the probable support of thirteen others. But it was not so. Burns was at that time going his own way, that was to take him away from the Social Democratic Federation and into the Liberal camp. Havelock Wilson of the Seamens Union was no Socialist and only looked like one when he was fighting the shipowners; he was more at home with the Liberals. The Lib/Labs had all committed themselves to the Liberal Party as a condition of electoral support.

Keir Hardie found himself as a party of one with the self-appointed task of challenging Parliament to care for all the people. Looking straight ahead he marched towards his objective challenging all who dared and cared to follow him.

Before he took his seat he had placed his freedom of action beyond any doubt by refusing financial help from Andrew Carnegie; the wealthy American employer, and then refusing £300 a year from two old ladies. The latter was tempting for as he said himself, 'To a man without a shilling, and the prospect of having to earn his living somehow, the offer had its practical advantages.' Members of Parliament were unpaid in those days.

Keir Hardie's arrival at the House of Commons caused a sensation. He would have taken the bus to Westminster, but in the event he arrived in a two horse brake supplied by some of his enthusiastic supporters. It had a trumpeter on the box and Keir was wearing – a cloth cap. The cloth cap was no doubt what we would call a 'deer stalker' in which he appears in early photographs. One report says that his wife, if not Keir himself, had never intended that he should attend the House in a cloth cap and had ordered a felt hat that did not arrive in time. Certainly he soon altered his garb to a dark suit and a hat, although never the frock coat and top hat that was de rigueur for a Tory or a Liberal.

For a poor man who spent much time travelling by train to speaking engagements and at meetings both indoors and out, a tweed suit was undoubtably a good choice particularly if it was his only one. And what could be more suitable for a long cold railway journey than that 'deer stalker' with those beautiful ear flaps.

On 12 August 1892 Parliament assembled preliminary to the formal opening of the new session. Business would commence when the Government had been formed and was scheduled for February 1893! Against precedent Hardie calmly rose to ask the Speaker whether an autumn session could be called to consider measures to improve the condition of the people. This proposal was ruled out of order but the fact was made that the 'Member for the Unemployed' had arrived.

Independent Labour Party (ILP)

Keir Hardie used the long recess to pursue the conception of creating a genuinely independent political party. A Conference was held in the Labour Institute, Bradford on 12 and 13 January 1893. One hundred and twenty-four delegates attended from England and Scotland, mainly representing the widespread local Labour and Socialist societies and clubs and some Trade Union Branches. There were no national representatives from the Trade Unions or the TUC. The objective was political not industrial.

They were not there to rubber stamp proposals. Each proposal was put from the floor of the Conference, amendments moved, votes taken. Keir Hardie was elected Chairman; probably no one else would have been able to unite these diverse characters under one banner. Among the delegates were:

Robert Smillie	later president of the Miners Federation and MP.
Joseph Burgess	Editor of the *Workmans Times*.
James Sexton	Liverpool dockers leader.
Pete Curran	of the Gas workers union.
Ben Tillett	London docker and later LCC Councillor and MP.
F.W. Jowett	one of the first Labour Councillors, later MP.
Katherine St. John Conway	later Mrs. Bruce Glasier, an eloquent speaker who equated Socialism with Christianity.
Robert Blatchford	Editor of *The Clarion* representing Manchester Socialists.
George Bernard Shaw	representing the Fabian Society.
H. Russell Smart	from Plymouth.
J. Shaw Maxwell	from the Scottish Labour Party, was at the end of the Conference elected secretary.

Proposals on the five main issues were put forward,

discussed and finally agreed.

1. OBJECT: To achieve the collective ownership and control of the means of production, distribution and exchange.

2. THE NAME: Scottish Labour Party delegates moved that the new organisation be called 'the Socialist Labour Party.' This was opposed by Ben Tillett who wished 'to capture the trade unionists.' He was well aware that 'socialism' could mean many things including what he called the 'harebrained chatterers and magpies of continental revolutionaries.' He did not want to put off trade unionists who were already fighting every day of the week the battles that the new political organisation was being formed to fight. An amendment that the new organisation be called the 'Independent Labour Party' was carried on a show of hands by a large majority.

3. ATTITUDE TO OTHER PARTIES: It was moved: 'That all members of the ILP pledged themselves to abstain from voting for any candidate for election to any representative body who is in any way a nominee of the Liberal, Liberal Unionist, or Conservative Party.' In most constituencies this would amount to voters boycotting the election as there would be no ILP candidate. Later this was superseded by a more realistic amendment, 'that in the absence of an ILP candidate, members should act as directed by their local branch.'

4. CONSTITUTION: The National Administrative Council elected at the end of the first day interpreted the will of the Conference that the ILP would have individual membership only, formed into branches. This eliminated the Fabians, the SDF and Trade Union branches. The Fabians promised future collaboration.

5. POLICY: The principal demands in the policy, after discussion and amendment were:

> A legal maximum of an eight hour working day.
> The abolition of overtime, piece-work and child labour.
> Public provision for the sick, disabled, widows and orphans.
> Unsectarian education.
> Tax on unearned income.
> Extending democratic rights.
> Democratising the system of government.

The writer William Stewart concluded:

> They had founded one of the most remarkable organisations that has ever existed in this or any other country   a political party and something more   a great social fellowship joining together in bonds of friendship all its adherents in every part of the land and forming a communion comparable to that of some religious fraternity whose members have taken vows of devotion to a common cause.

He published these words in 1921. I remember an incident that happened in, I believe, that year. My father cared deeply for people including, of course, his family but he was an undemonstrative man. In view of this it was remarkable that he always wore a red silk handkerchief in his breast pocket. It was a symbol of the ILP that he had joined at the age of sixteen in 1894. My mother had suggested I give him a new red handkerchief for his birthday, which I did. I would be about twelve years old. He opened the little parcel and gazed at it for a moment and then put his arm around me and kissed me. I do not remember this undemonstrative man kissing me at any other time.

It may be thought that William Stewart's words quoted above are extravagant. All I can say is that they would not have been thought so by my father, who had by that time enjoyed the fellowship of the ILP for twenty-seven years in Cumberland, London and Kent.

Member for the Unemployed

Keir Hardie had only two or three weeks to concentrate on the ILP before Parliament assembled on 7 February 1893. He had a powerful weapon in the *Labour Leader* that he had launched some years before with the support of the Scottish Labour Party. He continued to publish and edit it and the paper now became the mouthpiece of the ILP. The bulk of the Press published regular attacks on the Labour movement but the faithful could 'read all about it' in the *Labour Leader*, Robert Blatchford's *Clarion*, and a short lived but powerful paper the *Workmans Times* edited by Joseph Burgess.

The new Parliamentary Session was formally opened with the Queen's Speech setting out the business to be transacted. The Speech referred to the agricultural depression but not to industrial problems and not a word about the unemployed who were demonstrating daily only a few hundred yards away on the Embankment.

Keir Hardie rose to move an amendment that urged that this omission should be corrected to state that the Government would legislate promptly to provide help for the unemployed. The speech did not detail a whole string of reforms, it was certainly not putting forward an alternative to capitalism. It was a good radical parliamentary speech quoting Government statistics of 1,300,000 unemployed and 4,000,000 destitute. His intimate knowledge of the lives of these people and his passionate concern secured him a good hearing. He asked what had the unemployed to thank Her Majesty for in the speech that had been submitted to the house? They were left out as if they did not exist.

At the end of the ensuing debate the amendment was put to the vote. The Liberal Members of Parliament decided to ignore Keir Hardie's plea and back their Government's position by voting against his amendment calling for help to the unemployed. The Lib/Lab group were bound by their election undertakings and voted with them, John Burns refusing an offer to second Keir Hardie's amendment.

The Conservatives were put in an interesting position, they had never considered that the unemployed were the concern of themselves or the Government but they saw an opportunity to shake and conceivably defeat the Government by voting for the amendment. This they proceeded to do even though it meant supporting that man Keir Hardie.

The vote was: For the Amendment 109. Against 276.

Did the Liberal Government even consider accepting Keir Hardie's Amendment, it would have been morally right and surely better tactics. Members had voted for or against the Government without the slightest regard for the issue at stake. Again the unemployed were left out of the argument. Keir Hardie emerged as the man of principle and deserving the title 'Member for the Unemployed.'

Keir Hardie continued to harry the Government by constantly raising questions in the House that would bring to light the facts about destitution and discrimination. The House of Commons was being presented with a different picture of Britain. He asked whether more factory inspectors could be appointed and whether the Local Government Board could give information as to the number of unemployed in various industries. He enquired why some prison warders were dismissed without any reason being given. By what authority were troops and gunboats being sent to Hull to help shipowners to put down a strike by a Trade Union that was registered under an Act of Parliament? Had the shipowners refused all efforts at a compromise or conciliation? He elicited the information that out of thirty-nine Hull magistrates, four were shipowners, nineteen were shareholders in shipping and that none were working men.

Occasionally he put down a heavyweight question like this one:

I beg to ask the Chancellor of the Exchequer whether he contemplates, in connection with budget proposals for next year, such a rearrangement of the system of taxation as is known as graduated Income Tax, by means of which the contribution to the revenue would bear a relative proportion to income; also whether he will make such provisions in the Budget estimates next year as would enable the Local

Government Boards to make grants to any Board of Guardians, Town and County Councils, or committees of responsible citizens willing to acquire land or other property and to undertake the responsibility of organising the unemployed in home colonies and affording them the opportunity of providing the necessities of life for themselves and those dependent on them?

The land settlement scheme had been carried out by Crooks and Lansbury for Poplar. Hardie tied this to a realistic proposal for increased revenue by introducing graduated income tax.

ILP Defence and Attack

Keir Hardie now replied to attacks made on him by the Liberals in West Ham who were disturbed by the militancy of the ILP and were not prepared to support him on such issues as unemployment or the miners' eight hour day. His statement was forthright:

The ILP starts from the assumption that the worker should be as free industrially and economically as he is supposed to be politically, and that the land and the instruments of production should be owned by the community and should be used in producing the requisites to maintain a healthy and happy existence. The men who are to achieve these reforms must be under no obligation to either landlord or capitalist, or to any party or organisation representing their interests. Suppose for sake of argument that twenty members would be elected to Parliament who were nominally Labour Members but who owed their election to a compromise with the Liberals, what would be the effect upon their actions in the House of Commons? When questions affecting the interests of prosperity were at stake, or when they desired to take action to compel social action of a drastic character, the threat would always be hanging over them that unless they were obedient to the party whip and maintained party discipline they would be opposed.

In my own case, this threat has been held out so often that it is beginning to lose effect. I have no desire to hold the seat on sufferance and at the mercy of those who are not in agreement with me, and am quite prepared to be defeated when the election comes round. But I cannot agree to compromise my independence of action even the slightest degree.

The ILP was gathering strength throughout the country; leading figures joined including Ramsay MacDonald, Philip Snowden and Tom McCarthy. Tom Mann took over the Secretaryship and Ben Tillett was elected to the Council. Ramsay MacDonald wrote:

My dear Hardie. I am now making personal application for membership of the ILP. I have stuck to the Liberals up to now hoping that they might do something to justify the trust we have put in them. Attercliffe (a recent By Election where the local Liberals refused to accept a good working class candidate) came as a rude awakening, and I felt during that contest that it was quite impossible for me to maintain my position as a Liberal any longer. Calmer consideration has but strengthened that conviction, and if you now care to accept me amongst you I shall do what I can to support the ILP. Between you and me there was never any dispute as to objectives. What I could not accept was your methods. I have changed my opinion, Liberalism and more particularly local Liberal Associations, have definitely declared against Labour, and so I must accept the facts of the situation and candidly admit that the prophesies of the ILP relative to Liberalism have been amply justified. The time for conciliation has gone by and those of us who are earnest in our professions must definitely declare ourselves. I may say that in the event of elections, I shall place part of my spare time at the disposal of the Party, to do what works may seem good to you.

Yours very sincerely,   J.R. MacDonald.

This forthright statement of Keir Hardie's and the modest letter of Ramsay MacDonald are worth studying carefully; both had worked amicably with members of the Liberal Party but both had also met open hostility and contempt from the Liberals at local level. Keir Hardie had clashed with Liberal Members of Parliament who had used unemployment to force down the wages of their own employees. This was the turning-point; they might work with Liberals on specific matters from time to time but there would be no partnership.

On 31 March 1894 the *Labour Leader* became a weekly paper with Keir Hardie in addition to being the editor accepting the full management and financial responsibility. It was his voice to the Labour Movement, supplementing his public meetings all over the country and his work in the ILP and Parliament.

Explosion in Parliament

Three newsworthy events occurred in the month of June 1894:

23 June	An explosion at the Albion Colliery, Cilfynydd, South Wales, in which 260 men and boys lost their lives.
23 June	A child was born to the Duchess of York.
24 June	M. Carnot, the President of the French Republic was assassinated.

The second and third items were drawn to the attention of the House of Commons by Sir William Harcourt on behalf of the government; the first by Keir Hardie standing alone in the House.

When a vote of condolence was moved to the French

people on the assassination of their president, Keir Hardie enquired whether a vote of sympathy would also be moved to the relatives of the two hundred and sixty victims of the Welsh colliery disaster. 'Oh no', said Sir William in an off-hand tone of voice, 'I can dispose of that matter by saying that the House does sympathise with those poor people.' Keir Hardie's proposed amendment was ruled out of order. However he raised the matter again when the congratulatory address on the birth of the royal child came before the house. He moved that sympathy be expressed with the miners' relatives and detestation of a system that made the periodic sacrifice of men's lives inevitable. It was a passionate appeal. Keir Hardie knew the appalling safety record of the Albion pit; he had helped with the rescue work at a similar disaster at Udston colliery only six years before. He would be recalling vividly the scenes as they brought the bodies up while the wives and mothers wept and waited. He was outraged at the indifference of the House but he found not one member to support him; it was reported that the members 'howled and screamed and yelled.'

His intervention was treated as an insult to the Queen by the House and the Press. Cooler heads and warmer hearts might have sought to find a procedure whereby the loss of lite was recognised. The price miners continued to pay was recognised two generations later by a great grandson of the old Queen who visited South Wales and said, 'Something must be done.' Keir Hardie's challenge was not to the Queen but to the Government and the Members of the House of Commons who neither knew nor cared about miners, match girls, children working twelve hour shifts or starving unemployed. In the event of such a disaster today the Queen, Parliament and the whole nation would respond.

This occasion was not typical of Keir Hardie's experience in the House. The Members soon learnt to listen to him and respect him although not often to agree. He was once described as 'The first man of the workers who completely understood them, completely realised their plight and completely championed them. The first working man who having entered Parliament never deserted them, never turned back on a single principle.'

The day came when he put to the House the challenge to create a new order of society. Such was his integrity that they listened to him until nearly midnight. His resolution read:

> That considering the increased burden which the private ownership of land and capital is imposing upon the industrial and useful classes of the community, the poverty and destitution resulting from a competitive system of wealth production which aims primarily at profit making, the alarming growth of trusts and syndicates, and by reason of their great wealth to influence governments and plunge peaceful nations into war to serve their own interests, this House is of the opinion that such a state of matters is a menace to the well being of this nation and calls for legislation to remedy the same by inaugurating a Socialist Commonwealth founded upon the common ownership of land and capital, production for use and not for profit and equality of opportunity for every citizen.

He concluded his speech:

> Only by moral power can the necessary zeal and sacrifice be developed to carry our work through. I know of no movement for the good of the human race that has not been inspired by moral purpose. The best in life cannot be gained by looking after Number One. Socialism is a religious movement akin to the Reformation, and it is the only force able to inspire men

with the boundless devotion and utter disregard for personal interest or even personal safety. We are called upon to decide the questions propounded in the Sermon on the Mount as to whether we worship God or Mammon.

This was the faith of Keir Hardie that demanded that the House of Commons should care for Welsh miners and their widows and consider what sort of society that caring would build.

For the next two years Keir Hardie and his paper the *Labour Leader* were encouraging the ILP and trade union men to back his voice in Parliament with local campaigns to put pressure on their local MPs to do something about the unemployed. When Parliament reassembled Keir Hardie moved an amendment again calling on the Government to provide help for the unemployed. Sir William Harcourt this time was prepared and offered to set up a special committee to consider the question if Hardie would withdraw his amendment. This was the first time that the Government had admitted that the unemployed were in any way their concern. A Press correspondent reported on the scene as Keir Hardie rose to speak:

Members poured in from every part, until every bench had its full quota of Members, whilst a crowd stood below the bar and another crowded behind the Speaker's chair. Both front benches were crowded with Ministers and ex Ministers and the attention of the House was kept unbroken from start to finish.

Keir Hardie replied, 'If the Government can find the committee and make an interim report I will withdraw the amendment.' Throughout the debate Keir Hardie was being treated as seriously in the House as if he was the leader of an opposition party of one hundred members instead of only one. Sir William Harcourt's capitulation was received with cheers. It was a step towards Keir Hardie's vision of a House of Commons that would be concerned with the lot of all the people.

In the House the weakness of the Liberal Party continued to be exposed and in July the government suffered defeat and a General Election was called.

The General Election of 1895 saw the Liberals routed and some leading figures such as Sir William Harcourt defeated. The ILP fielded twenty-eight candidates. None were elected, Keir Hardie losing his seat at West Ham. The ILP had entered the contest ill-equipped both in organisation and finance. In spite of this three candidates each received over four thousand votes, but in other constituencies there was little more than a token campaign and several good men received less than four hundred votes.

The dedicated ILP stalwarts regarded the results as a propaganda success, the average vote for their candidates being 1592. Had they been able to field a candidate in every constituency and achieve the same rate of support they would have secured one million votes. Were there a million people out there waiting for a chance to support the reconstruction of society? Even if there were, where were the resources to come from to reach them? The paid-up membership of the ILP at this time was little more than ten thousand.

In the long term the vision was to build a classless order of society, a Cooperative Commonwealth. In the short term it was to secure better conditions for the workers, the old, the children, the sick and the unemployed. Many good men in the Trade Unions were working to meet the short term need but were not prepared to commit themselves to a long term vision that they did not understand. Could they not work together? The ILP was aiming for the heights, but surely it was wrong to spurn those that toiled on the lower slopes.

Between 1895 and 1900 four by-elections were fought by leading ILP men Tom Mann (twice), Keir Hardie and Pete Curran. All were lost although polling substantial votes. They opposed a Liberal in all four elections and a Conservative in three. The Social Democratic Federation fought two by-elections in this period, in both cases getting less than three hundred votes. An effective machine had yet to be forged to mobilise the working class vote.

America

In 1895 Keir Hardie received an invitation from the American Labour Day Committee to attend the Chicago Labour Congress on 2 September. This fitted in with a determination he had long had to strengthen links with the trade unions and other labour organisations in America, Australia and New Zealand.

He set off from Liverpool a few days after his thirty-seventh birthday with an old friend Frank Smith who had come into the Socialist movement from being a principal organiser of social work for the Salvation Army. The Merseyside socialists organised a great demonstration on the quayside and not content with that, they chartered a tug on which a crowd of enthusiasts cheered and sang the liner *Campania* on its way. Every passenger learnt that the demonstration was for the benefit of the Labour leader Keir Hardie. He was asked to address the passengers in the course of the voyage. He talked about society using the different classes of accommodation on the ship, from first class to steerage as an illustration. He preached the same socialism to them as he preached wherever he was invited.

Passengers were putting back their watches an hour each day so as to be right when they arrived in New York. Keir did not alter his so that he could look at his watch and think about what his wife and the children were doing each hour of the day.

In New York they mingled with the early morning line of hungry men waiting for a free distribution of bread outside the Vienna bakery and at night they wandered through China Town. They were guests at the exclusive Manhattan Club and all sections of the Labour movement joined together to honour them.

Keir Hardie was the chief speaker at the great Labour Day demonstration in Chicago. They travelled to Woodstock to visit a trade union leader in prison, and crossed the States to San Francisco visiting many cities, mining areas and remote rural areas along the way.

From Butte City they visited an Indian encampment in a buggy friends had supplied for them. At this point they were down to their last dollar, a remittance from Chicago having failed to arrive. Driving along in the buggy Keir heard a strange and familiar sound, 'Do you hear that music?', he asked the driver. 'That ain't no music', was the reply, 'that's the Scotch pipes.' They drove to the sound of the pipes and found a saloon and its pipe-playing host MacDonald. The outcome of this was a hastily called meeting at the Opera House for Keir to speak. A profit of seventy-five dollars from the meeting was handed to Keir. 'And that', said Keir, 'was how Providence came to the rescue at Butte City.'

Everywhere Keir Hardie addressed meetings and conferences and conferred with Trade Union, Socialist and Civic leaders. In San Francisco he met the Mayor, Mr. Bryan, who had made millions of dollars out of silver mining, his aim was to establish bimetallism as a basis for currency. He offered Keir one hundred thousand dollars (about twenty thousand pounds) if he would advocate bimetallism to the ILP. Mr. Bryan could not understand how a poor man like Keir Hardie could refuse such an offer, but of course he did.

Europe

The concept of 'workers of the world unite' was very much in the air throughout Europe. It led in 1889 to the formation of the Second Socialist International and Keir Hardie attended the Congress in Paris. Farm and factory workers, miners and dockers throughout Europe had the same basic needs and the same hopes and fears. Properly organised, their sheer weight of numbers could change the world. But how, and what sort of world would they build?

By the date of a later Congress Keir Hardie attended in Amsterdam he had been the architect of a workers' movement that mustered enough votes to send him to a democratically elected Parliament. Few of the delegates saw much hope of following this path in their own countries. There was a fundamental division between these delegates who wanted to build democracy for all the people and those that wanted workers to take revolutionary action to seize power for their class. Each group took their divisions to the point of moving a resolution to exclude the rival group from the International. Keir Hardie opposed a split; he was almost alone among them in seeing what they had in common. What mattered most was their understanding and concern about the exploitation of millions of their fellow men, their determination to change all this and above all to prevent war. They could find new truths together.

On his return from Amsterdam Keir Hardie published an 'Indictment of the Class War' in the *Labour Leader*. He opposed the class war dogma because it led workers to look 'only outside themselves for the causes that perpetuated their misery.' In this country the workers already had the political power to free themselves. They must use it. In his words 'it is a degradation of the socialist movement to drag it down to the level of a mere struggle for supremacy between two contending factions.' Keir Hardie also at this time set out his own belief about the way forward for Socialism in Britain:

> Wherever free Parliamentary institutions exist, and where Socialism has attained the status of being recognised as a Party, dogmatic absolutism is giving way before the advent of a more practical set of working principles. The schoolman is being displaced by the statesman. No hard and fast rule can be laid down for the application of the new methods, but generally speaking, where the Socialist propaganda has so far succeeded as to have built up a strong party in the state, and where the ties that kept the older parties together have so far been dissolved that there are no longer an effective Reform Party remaining, there the Socialists may be expected to lend their aid in erecting a new combination of such progressive forces as give an intellectual assent to Socialism, and are prepared to co-operate in waging war against reaction and in rallying the forces of democracy. When this can be done so as in no way impair the freedom of action of a Socialist party, or to blur the vision of the Socialist ideal, it would appear as if the movement had really no option but to accept its share of the responsibility of guiding the State. Then, just in proportion as Socialism grows, so will the influence of the

representatives in the national councils increase, and the world may wake up some morning to find Socialism has come.

Meanwhile he was engaged in fighting for the right of free speech at home. The outdoor meeting was the main weapon of the ILP branches all over the country. Local speakers often supplemented by leading speakers, attracted large audiences, Tom Mann, Joseph Burgess, Keir Hardie and women such as Mrs. Bruce Glasier, Enid Stacy and Caroline Martyn. Generally the meetings were held at long established meeting places, commons, parks and squares. Their success attracted opposition and attempts were made to deny the ILP the right to use these places. One of the most famous cases concerned Boggart Hole Clough, part of a Manchester City park. The Parks Committee gave notice prohibiting meetings on the grounds that they caused an obstruction. The ILP nevertheless continued with the meetings and as a result the speakers were brought before the magistrates and fined. Two refused to pay the fine and were each sent to prison for a month. The publicity increased the popularity of the meetings and the magistrates resorted to adjourning cases without passing sentence. Keir Hardie was called before the magistrates and gave notice that he would call 473 witnesses. In the end the Council amended their rules and the right of free speech and assembly was restored.

Keir Hardie and many like him continued an incredible round of activity. He once set down the details of a fortnight's work in winter, from midday when he left his home in Scotland:

Nov. 17 Left home 12 noon; reached London 10.45 pm.

18 Office work. Open air meeting in West Ham at night.
19 Left London 07.15 am.; opened bazaar at Halifax 2.30; spoke at Honley at 8 pm.
20 Halifax Labour Church two meetings.
21 Opened bazaar at 3; addressed meeting at Yeadon at 8 pm.
22 Addressed meeting at Mexboro; 3 hours in train.
23 Mexboro to Kettering in train 3 hours. Feet wet trudging through snow. Meeting at 8 pm.
24 Kettering to London. Meeting in Canning Town.
25 London to Pendlebury, 5 hours. Two committees.
26 National Administration Council, 10 to 5. Conference Social 5 to 11.
27 10.30 meeting at Eccles; 3 pm ditto at Pendlebury; 6 pm ditto ditto.
28 Meeting at Walkden.
29 Committee in Manchester at 4. Conference with Oldham branches at 8.
30 12.45 midnight started home. Number of letters received and answered 75.

In addition he had his *Labour Leader* articles to write varying from four to a dozen columns weekly. Much of his writing was done in the comfortless third class railway carriages, meals were as irregular as some of the beds. He took only bare expenses, in return he gave all he had. His writing in the *Labour Leader* was not bread and butter stuff; he set himself definite objectives and fought a whole series of campaigns in the paper to expose the harsh conditions imposed on men and women and children working in industry.

In 1889 workers at the Shawfield Chemical Works at Rutherglen near Glasgow appealed for help to the *Labour Leader*. The men worked twelve hours a day, seven days a week, without a meal break for threepence and fourpence an hour. The work involved the manufacture of chrome potash, that led to many workers suffered from incurable skin diseases, respiratory and digestive illness. This case was not unusual in industry, what made it special was the character of the head of the firm Lord Overtoun, a Liberal. He was noted for religious and charitable work giving a huge sum every year to Christian missionary and charitable work. His factory worked a continuous process – men, women and children worked long hours seven days a week. The money this man gave away was the profit made out of the wretched men and women he employed. That he could treat them as he did and involve the name of Jesus raised Keir Hardie's wrath. The *Labour Leader* published all the facts and pulled no punches in a series of weekly articles later published as a pamphlet. Pressure was put on the printer not to print any more references to Lord Overtoun. The paper appeared with a blank page but another printer was found and the story continued in the next edition. Gradually Lord Overtoun gave way, most Sunday work was stopped and conditions improved. The challenge to Christians to live what they talk about continued to be hammered home in the *Labour Leader*. Do unto others as you would they should do unto you.

South African War

War seemed imminent in South Africa when on 9 September 1899 the National Administrative Council of the ILP met under the chairmanship of Keir Hardie. The following statement was issued by the Council:

> The National Administrative Council of the ILP protests against the manner in which the Government, by the tenor of their despatches and their war-like presentations, have made a peaceful settlement difficult with the Transvaal Republic. The policy of the Government can be explained only on the supposition that the intentions have been to provoke a war of conquest to secure complete control in the interests of unscrupulous exploitation.
>
> A war of aggression is, under any circumstances, an outrage on the moral sense of a civilised community and in the present instance particularly so, considering the sordid character of the real objectives aimed at.
>
> It is especially humiliating to the democratic instincts of this country that ulterior and unworthy motives should be hidden under the pretence of broadening political liberties....
> We also protest against the action of the press and the bulk of the leading politicians in strengthening the criminal conduct of the Government by misleading the public and rousing the passion for war, and we express the hope that it may not yet be too late for the manhood of the nation to prevent the outrage upon the conscience of our common humanity.

Five weeks later war broke out. The press, with the exception of the Manchester Guardian among leading newspapers, set out to whip up war fever. Conservatives supported their Government and the war, Liberals temporised; only a few courageous men in either party spoke out in favour of a peaceful settlement.

The ILP now issued a further statement:

> In view of the terrible sacrifice of life, widespread suffering, and the enormous destruction of property, which the present

war has entailed, and must further entail if it is prosecuted to the bitter end, we recommend that the Government of Great Britain and the South African Republic should at once declare the terms of peace that would be acceptable to them, so that it would be possible for either the Government by acceptance of them, now or at any time during the course of the war, to bring hostilities to a close. We believe that such a decision would be in harmony with the proposal agreed at the recent Peace Conference at the Hague; and that it would be approved by the people of our land and every civilised land, and that, in addition to probably bringing a speedy end to the present war, it would form a precedent that might save this and other countries from war in the future.

Keir Hardie wrote extensively in the *Labour Leader*, tracing the history of the Dutch settlements, the discovery of gold, the arrival of British speculators and summarised the situation:

The war is a capitalist war. The British merchant hopes to secure markets for his goods, the investor an outlet for his capital, the speculator more fools out of whom to make money, and the mining companies cheaper labour and increased dividends.

The ILP was isolated in its proposals for a peaceful settlement. Expectations of a quick victory disappeared as the months wore on amid defeats and bloodshed. A quarter of a million British troops were eventually deployed.

On Christmas Eve, Silas Hocking the novelist, writing from the National Liberal Club, sent the following letter to the press:

Sir, There are many people who think with myself, that the time has come when some organised attempt should be made by those who believe in the New Testament to put a stop to the inhuman slaughter that is going on in South Africa – a slaughter that is not only a disgrace to civilisation, but which brings our Christianity into utter contempt. Surely sufficient blood has been shed. No one can any longer doubt the courage or the skill of either of the combatants, but why prolong the strife? Cannot we in the name of the Prince of Peace cry 'Halt!' and seek some peaceful settlement of the questions in dispute? As the greater, and as we think, the more Christian nation, we should cover ourselves with honour in asking for an armistice and seeking a settlement by peaceful means. We can win no honour by fighting, whatever the issues may be. In order to test the extent of the feeling to which I have given expression and with the view to holding a conference in London at an early date, I shall be willing to receive the names of anyone who may be willing to cooperate.

Canon Scott Holland preaching in St. Paul's Cathedral said:

We should humiliate ourselves for the blundering recklessness with which we entered the war, and the insolence and arrogance which blinded us so utterly. Let there be no more vainglory, no more braggart tongues, and let us at the beginning of the New Year find our true understanding.

Keir Hardie and the ILP associated themselves with the 'Stop the War Campaign', which held successful meetings in most of the main cities in the face of widespread and often violent opposition. The prevailing mood was that with a quarter of a million of our troops deployed in South Africa we must fight on to win. Although what 'to win' involved was not explained. In the famous phrase of Lord Carrington at the time, 'We must all stop thinking until the war is over.' To Keir Hardie and men like him who could not stop thinking, the war was like a colliery disaster writ large with women weeping over their dead.

Realignment

Meanwhile the whole question of the future of working class politics was being looked at again. The ILP was a success, it had developed socialist thinking and created a band of brothers but a broader front had to be constructed if Parliamentary and Local Government seats were to be won. The idealism of the ILP needed to be wedded to the mass organisation of the Trade Unions and Scotland led the way.

On 6 January 1900 a conference was held in the Free Gardeners Hall, Edinburgh. There were 226 delegates present:

Trade unions	116
Trades councils	29
Cooperatives	28
ILP	34
SDF	19

Robert Smillie, of the Scottish Miners, was in the chair, with Keir Hardie and Joseph Burgess also on the platform. These three had played major parts in the setting up of the ILP in 1893. The following resolution was carried by the conference:

> Recognising that no real progress has been made with those important measures of social and industrial reforms that are necessary for the comfort and well being of the working classes, and further recognising that neither of the two parties can or will effect these reforms, this Conference is of the opinion that the only means by which such reforms can be obtained is by having direct independent working class representation in the House of Commons and in local administrative bodies, and hereby pledges itself to secure that end as a logical sequence for the possession of political

power by the working classes.

It is comparatively easy to gather twelve like-minded people together and agree on one thing. Just a plank not a platform. If you gather twelve people together to get them to agree on twelve items, twelve planks for a platform, then you have got a problem. If you tackle it, as you must, you may provide an entertaining spectacle for those who have never tried to make democracy work, but you have to try. The capacity to do it depends upon what you believe about the nature of man. It has to start with respect for the other man, you have to believe that there is good in him and that whether he does good or ill in the business in hand depends as much on you as it does on him. If you believe that both can do better, both can change, then you have a chance.

During 1884 to 1900 we can identify five main points of view:

Some Conservatives
That progress in terms of better health care, education, housing, and working conditions for the workers were neither necessary nor practical.

A few Conservatives and all Liberals
That progress in these fields is necessary and practical and should be achieved step by step within the capitalist system.

Members of the ILP and the Fabians
That progress in these fields is necessary and practical and should be achieved step by step leading eventually to the replacing of capitalism by a classless Cooperative Commonwealth.

Members of the Social Democratic Federation
That progress in these fields is not practical to any meaningful degree without eliminating capitalism and transferring power to the workers.

Most of the rest (probably the majority)
There is nothing that people like us can do about the state of society.

Working class people in this period could be found in all those groups except the first. People who regarded themselves as working class were the overwhelming majority of the population. If working class people could work together, even with the limited franchise of those days, they could win power through the ballot box.

Labour Representation Committee

Towards the end of the nineteenth century the Liberal Party retained the political support of most of the members of the craft unions in England and Wales although disenchantment with the Liberals' performance on labour questions was growing. Keir Hardie and others had for some years been campaigning at Trade Union Congress and in the country for independent labour representation. There was eventually a breakthrough at the 1899 Annual Congress when the Parliamentary Committee of the TUC was instructed by a majority vote to set up a joint committee with the Cooperative and Socialist bodies to pursue the question of independent labour representation.

This joint committee hammered out a set of proposals to be put before a delegate conference. However the Parliamentary Committee, without consulting the other members of the Joint Committee, created some problems by revising the proposals before sending them out as the agenda for the Conference.

The Conference met on 27 February 1900 at the Memorial Hall, Farringdon Street, London. There were 129 delegates from the trade unions and three socialist societies. The Trade Union Congress had facilitated the Conference but was not itself a party to it, the trade union delegates representing their individual unions. The bodies represented were:

> Trade Union delegates representing 568,000 members.
> Independent Labour Party (ILP) 'Brotherhood of Man' Socialists.
> Social Democratic Federation (SDF) 'Class war' Socialists.
> Fabian Society self-appointed socialist 'Think Tank.'

Notable absentees were the Cooperative Societies, the textile unions and most of the miners' unions.

There were tremendous difficulties ahead; some trade union delegates were actually not in favour of independent representation at all; certainly the majority were not socialists. The SDF regarded all non-socialists as 'the enemy.' There were powerful individuals present. Ben Tillett who had founded his union was an ILP man, Will Thorne who had also founded his union was a SDF man, Alexander Wilkie founder of his union was a Liberal. They had a common interest in getting a strong united voice in Parliament but could they agree on a framework for a new political party before this fateful day was out? Astonishing as it may seem they did, and these three men were among those who stood for Parliament in the 1906 General Election under the banner of the Labour Representation Committee.

In Keir Hardie's words:

> The object of the Conference was... to ascertain whether organisations representing different ideals could find an immediate and common ground of action, leaving each organisation free to maintain and propagate its own theory in its own way; the object of the Conference was to secure a united Labour vote in support of Labour candidates and cooperation amongst them on Labour questions when returned.

The procedure for the Conference was inevitably complex; little of the document before them was acceptable as it stood. It had to be virtually rewritten section by section by means of amendments moved from the floor, discussed and voted on. However the chairman and the delegates were old hands at democratic procedure and if anyone could do it, they could.

The unenviable task of taking the chair at the conference fell to W.C. Steadman of the Barge Builders, the Lib/Lab Member of Parliament for Stepney. He was a man who had done good work on the London County Council with Ben Tillett, John Burns and Ramsay MacDonald (all members of the Conference). Like them he understood what representing Labour was all about.

Early on in the Conference James Macdonald (Secretary of the London Trades Council, not to be confused with J. Ramsay MacDonald) for the SDF put forward as an amendment that 'recognition of the class war' be built into the constitution. He was strongly opposed by trade unionists such as Ben Tillett and his proposal was inevitably defeated.

Alexander Wilkie representing the shipwrights put forward as an amendment a reasonably acceptable list of objectives to be included and this was carried, but later when a second amendment was moved by Keir Hardie on the same section it was, by agreement, withdrawn. Keir Hardie's amendment was the key statement at the Conference:

> ... to establish a distinct Labour group in Parliament, who shall have their own whips, and agree on their policy, which must embrace a readiness to cooperate with any party which for the time being may be engaged in promoting legislation in the direct interest of labour and equally ready to associate themselves with any party in opposing measures having an opposite tendency....

Wilkie's withdrawal of his proposals gave a lead to the other Trade Union representatives and Keir Hardie's amendment was carried without dissent.

Each of the affiliated bodies would continue with their own organising and propaganda work, but the new body would take on the task of putting forward Parliamentary candidates. The way was clear and the new party came into being forthwith. Its title was to be the 'Labour Representation Committee' although it was soon commonly called the Labour Party that became its official title after the 1906 General Election.

The Conference set up an Executive Committee of twelve members, the number of seats allocated to each affiliated body and the members appointed were:

The ILP   2 delegates   Keir Hardie
                           and James Parker.
The SDF   2 delegates   James Macdonald
                           and Harry Quelch.

The Fabians 1 delegate   F.R. Pease.

The Trade Unions   Frederick Rogers

        7 delegates   (Vellum Bookbinders)

                   Thomas Greenall

                   (Lancashire Miners)

                   Richard Bell

                   (Amalgamated Society of

                     Railway Servants)

                   Pete Curran

                   (Gas Workers and General

                     Labourers)

                   Allan Gee

                   (Yorkshire Textile

                     Workers)

                   Alexander Wilkie

                   (Shipwrights)

                   John Hodge

                   (Scottish Steel Smelters).

The three Socialist societies on the executive had between them five delegates out of twelve, in addition at least two of the Trade Union representatives were ILP members. So the Socialists were over-represented in terms of numbers but not in proportion to their contribution to the ideology and framework of the new party. To complete the business James Ramsay MacDonald of the ILP was elected Secretary.

The ILP, the SDF and the Fabians now had a mandate to cooperate with the Trade Union Movement and the opportunity to influence its one and a half million members. The ILP had accepted that they could not win power without them, the challenge was to maintain their own integrity as Socialists and at the same time work for common objectives with the trade union men. The SDF could not accept this challenge; they saw anyone who was not a socialist as their enemy, they later withdrew from the Labour Representation Committee. This was sad; they had some fine men in their ranks.

The Conference was a remarkable success; it is doubtful if anyone expected so much. There was plain speaking and there were differences but throughout there was a spirit of purpose and comradeship. The intervention by the SDF only served to demonstrate the gulf between them and the great majority of the delegates. They even failed in the atmosphere of this Conference to carry along some of their own members among the delegates, notably Will Thorne.

It is difficult ninety years later, when moral motives have been largely overlaid by self-interest, to understand that at this Conference the delegates saw the problems in society that their movement would tackle as fundamentally moral problems. Right and wrong. So a socialist speaker in those days at a mass meeting would expose and condemn the evil of the exploitation of children in the factories, and in the same speech expose and condemn the evils of drunkenness that led to the exploitation of children in the home. Both were wrong, and an employer or father stood in both cases condemned and must change his ways. The delegates were tough self-educated men who knew hardship and privation; many knew what it meant to share with their neighbour their last loaf of bread.

It was this ability to care and share that convinced them that humanity was capable of building a new society. They had founded a moral movement.

So Ramsay MacDonald went home to set up the office

of the LRC in a room in his flat at 3 Lincolns Inn Fields and to start writing to ask the trade unions to confirm their membership and send their affiliation fee of ten shillings per thousand members. At this figure it was not surprising that in September it was decided to defer the question of an honorarium to the Secretary for his services. At the end of the first year forty-one unions had affiliated with a membership of 353,070 members. A disappointment was that the Cooperative Congress in June decided not to affiliate. *The Clarion* wrote:

> At last there is a United Labour party, or perhaps it is safer to say, a little cloud, no bigger than a man's hand, which may grow into a United Labour Party.

Back to Parliament

In September 1900 a general election was called and all was confusion. Hardly any Labour candidates had been selected and the LRC was not yet in a position to give much practical help and still less financial. The problem of mounting any sort of campaign was difficult enough but this was to be known as the 'Khaki election' for the South African war was the main issue in everyone's minds. Socialists and some Liberals such as David Lloyd George faced physical violence as they tried to put the case for peace and cooperation to crowds of angry opponents. This issue was going to lose Labour a lot of votes. Most socialists and notably the ILP were opposed to the war regarding it as military support for financiers and exploiters, but patriotic fervour had been stirred up by the newspapers and they carried the bulk of the people with them.

The massive trade union forces that could have turned

the scales were not yet mobilised behind the ILP only five LRC candidates received official trade union backing at this general election. Eight more were sponsored by the ILP, one by the SDF and one by the ILP and the SDF together. Only fifteen seats were to be fought under the LRC banner.

Keir Hardie had not been selected for any constituency when the dissolution of Parliament was announced. Selection of a candidate was primarily a local matter and involved agreement between the ILP and the trade unions. Keir Hardie was being considered for both Preston and Merthyr Tydfil. Bruce Glasier, now chairman of the ILP, wrote to the local ILP Secretary in Wales Llewellyn Francis:

> .... The National Administrative Council meets on Monday at Derby.... Among the most important things that we shall have to come to some conclusion upon, is the constituency which Keir Hardie ought to be advised to contest. We all feel that Hardie has a claim to the best constituency that we can offer him, and we feel that it is of the utmost importance to the Party that he should be returned. Hardie himself does not view his being returned to Parliament as a matter of much moment, and he is only anxious that at least he should fight where a worthy vote would be obtained. But I am sure you will agree with us that if any single man is to be returned, that man should be Hardie. I am therefore going to ask you to kindly inform me as frankly as possible what you would think would be Hardie's chances were he to contest Merthyr, and especially what you think would be the attitude of the trade unionists and miners' leaders. Hardie has himself a warm heart towards a South Wales seat — or rather, if you will, contest — but I am anxious that there should be a reasonable hope of a very large vote, if not actual success, before we consent to him standing. I am sure, therefore, you will give me your sincere opinion on the matter....

However the negotiations in Merthyr with the trade unions dragged on and Keir Hardie accepted the invitation to stand at Preston. No sooner had he done so than a meeting at Merthyr with the trade unionists gave him full support. Keir Hardie fought both seats and lost at Preston. The Merthyr poll was actually a day later so he travelled down for the last day of the campaign there to find scenes of wild enthusiasm. Merthyr in those days was a two-seat constituency and there were three candidates. Keir Hardie himself, two Liberals and no Conservative. One Liberal D.A. Turner (later Lord Rhondda) was a popular candidate and an opponent of the South African war and he was certain to get one seat. Could Keir Hardie split the Liberals and win the second seat?

When it was all over Keir wrote:

> I have dim notions of weary hours in a train, great enthusiastic open air crowds in the streets of Preston and thereafter oblivion. Jack Penny tells me that my opening performance in the afternoon included almost continuous speaking from three o'clock till eight, with a break of an hour for tea....

Then he describes the counting of the votes at Merthyr:

> The Drill Hall; the general presiding officers; the anxious faces of the watchers at the table as the voting urns were emptied and their contents sorted. Joe Burgess, confident from the start; Francis strained to a tension that threatened rupture; Di Davies, drawn 'twixt hope and fear; the brothers Parker, moved to the cavernous depths of their being; ... at length came the figures, and Di gave vent to his feelings....

D.A. Turner	8598	} Elected
J. Keir Hardie	5745	
M. Prichard Morgan	4004	

A great cheering crowd. A march to a weird song whilst perched on the shoulders of some stalwart colliers, I trying vainly to not to look undignified. A chair helped considerably. That night from the hotel window, in response to cries loud and long continued, I witnessed a sight I never hoped to see this side of the pearly gates. My wife was making a speech to the delighted crowd.

I remember as a boy some twenty years after these events my father standing for the local council where no socialist had ever succeeded. A customer in my father's little shop told him that he had no chance. My father bet him a new hat that he would get 1500 votes and as no candidate had ever got into four figures the bet was promptly accepted. My father had never bet before and although he won the election by a huge majority he lost the bet by twenty-five votes. I was at the declaration of the poll with my Uncle John. I had never encountered such excitement even when our local football team scored a goal in a cup tie. At one stage we were pressed up against a motor car that had got trapped by the crowd; suddenly my uncle grabbed my arm with a look of anguish on his face, he had been shouting so much that he had completely lost his voice and could not cry out as the wheel of the car rolled onto his foot.

So I try to imagine that night in the Welsh valleys where they could not only shout, they could sing. The celebrations continued for several weeks as Keir Hardie was feted throughout the land, first of all in the Town Hall in Cumnock and an emotional reunion with many of the miners he had worked with twenty years before in Ayrshire. Alex Barrowman speaking for them paid tribute to Keir Hardie:

... had he cared to turn his talents to personal advantage he might today have been a wealthy man. Liberalism or Conservatism would have paid a big price for his services had they been for sale, whilst he might have found an easy life as a writer for the ordinary press. But he was not built that way. He had all his life been creating agencies through which the spirit of democracy might find expression, and had been content to sow what others might reap. Twenty years ago he might have found a snug berth as Secretary to some old established Union, instead of which, he came to Ayrshire where the men were not organised and established a union that had now nine thousand members. Not finding any newspapers representative of his opinions, he had started one, and the Labour Leader was now a recognised power. Seeing through what he conceived to be the hollowness of political parties, he set out to found a Party of his own, and had succeeded, for the Labour Party was now a reality....

Then to Glasgow and a tremendous meeting at the City Hall crowded with Socialists, Trade Union men and Cooperators who had come to honour him. The following week a similar enthusiastic gathering at the Free Trade Hall in Manchester, and then a banquet in London and triumphal tour through his constituency. Finally back to the family in Ayrshire to rest and gather his strength for another lonely battle in the House of Commons.

For lonely it was. He tried to get the Lib/Lab members particularly the miners to join with him and offered John Burns the leadership of such a group. All to no avail. Even Richard Bell who had stood under the LRC banner accepted the Liberal whip. He saw some humour in the situation that when the party leaders summoned their members to Parliament, no one summoned Keir Hardie.

On 23 April 1901 Keir Hardie won a place in the private members ballot giving him the opportunity to put a resolution before the House. He was last on the list and he rose to speak at twenty-five minutes to twelve and the House would adjourn at midnight. Keir Hardie had twenty-five minutes in which to say whatever he wanted to say on a subject of his choosing: What would you say? He spoke to the following proposal:

> That considering the increasing burden which the private ownership of land and capital is imposing upon the industrious and useful classes of the community, the poverty and destitution and general moral and physical deterioration resulting from a competitive system of wealth production which aims primarily at profit making, alarming growth of trusts and syndicates, able by reason of their great wealth to influence governments and plunge peaceful nations into war to serve their own interests, this House is of the opinion that such a state of matters is a menace to the well being of the Realm and calls for legislation designed to remedy the same by inaugurating a Socialist Commonwealth founded upon the common ownership of land and capital, production for use and not for profit, and equality of opportunity for every citizen.

He ended his speech to the House with these words:

> Socialism, by placing the land and instruments of production in the hands of the community, will eliminate only the idle and useless classes at both ends of the scale. The millions of toilers and business men do not benefit from the present system. We are called upon to decide the question propounded in the Sermon on the Mount as to whether we will worship God or Mammon. The last has not been heard of this movement either in the House or in the Country, for as surely as Radicalism democratised the system of government politically in the last century, so will Socialism democratise the industrialism of the country in the coming century.

Keir Hardie remained a powerful, if isolated, figure in

Parliament and continued to bring the needs of working people to the floor of the House of Commons. The Liberals were ineffective and the Lib/Labs had their hands tied.

In the country the strike of railwaymen against the Taff Vale Railway Company created a crisis as court cases and finally an appeal to the House of Lords struck at the very heart of the trade union movement. Together these various actions made trade unions and their officials individually liable for damages resulting from industrial strikes and other industrial action.

The matter reached the floor of the House largely as a result of extreme lobbying by members of the trade unions. Wentworth Beaumont, a radical liberal member, proposed and Richard Bell seconded, 'That legislation is necessary to prevent workmen being placed by judge-made law in a position inferior to that intended by Parliament in 1875.' Haldane, Asquith, Hardie and others called for an enquiry into the laws of conspiracy and picketing. The proposal was defeated by 203 votes to 174. Parliament was not even prepared to examine the position.

In the short term it appeared that the unions were now defenceless in their endeavours to support their members against exploitation, but these events served to force the minds of the unions on the need for labour representation in Parliament. The affiliated membership of the LRC increased:

1900	232,000
1901	383,773
1902	626,613
1903	847,315

Keir Hardie continued his punishing schedule, setting out on long train journeys most week ends, usually fitting in two or three meetings. He was in great demand as a speaker in the Cooperative Movement, the Temperance Movement and the Free Churches. He spoke to each of them not as a proselytising socialist but as a man fully identified with their Movement, recognising them as essential partners in creating a new society. He reminded the Cooperative Movement that they were part of an even greater Movement, the establishment of the cooperative shop not only gave workers and their families better and cheaper food but gave them confidence and self-reliance in their fight for better conditions. He spoke of the rapidly growing development by municipalities of housing, transport, and other services as another way in which communities were meeting their own needs.

A new society would not be imposed, it was already being built as they lived out what they talked about. His knowledge and understanding of what they were trying to do inspired them to do better. He had the breadth of vision and the warmth of heart to include them all; the brotherhood of man could not be an exclusive brotherhood.

In July 1901 Keir Hardie was ill and had to take to his bed. This was a new experience for him although he was back in action within a week. Every day he was busy with visitors, deputations, and committees. The *Labour Leader* alone would be a full time job for any ordinary man and he had no secretary to help him cope with his crowded life and extensive correspondence. Some of his friends were getting most concerned for his health and pressed him to take a long holiday.

January 1902 saw him facing a different stress. His

daughter Agnes was dangerously ill and he spent time in his home helping to nurse her back to health. In April his mother and father died within an hour of each other. They had known that they were not long for this world. Keir wrote:

> These two talked about death as if it were an everyday incident in their lives. They did so without emotion... had it been a visit to Glasgow, three miles distant, they could have not been more concerned.... They had fought life's battles together, fought them nobly and well, and it was meet that they should enter the void together.

In spirit they had also fought all Keir's battles with him, angry when he was attacked or misrepresented, bursting with pride at his achievements. He had always accepted David Hardie as his father and was devoted to his mother who had fought and sacrificed for him for so long.

Keir Hardie created for himself a new London home. He found a large room in Nevill's Court, Fetter Lane, a quiet backwater off Fleet Street; it was close to the Labour Leader office, twenty minutes walk from Westminster and the rent was six shillings and sixpence a week. He had it divided into sitting room, bedroom and kitchen with matchboard partitions. It had a long window sill flower box where he grew primroses, leeks from Wales and gowan transplanted from his Scottish garden.

Surrounded by his books, mementoes and many photographs of friends, some long departed, he would not have exchanged it for a palace. It was to be his London home for the rest of his life. Here he would entertain his friends, miners from Wales and Scotland, poets and painters, sculptors and writers, visitors from many countries and, of course, members of his family from

Scotland. He treasured, too, the times when he could be alone. In his words, 'Yes, my mansion is perfect. The spirits of the living and the dead whom I serve are here.'

Keir Hardie at Nevill's Court.

In June 1902 there was a by-election in the Lancashire constituency that consists of a string of towns and villages in the heart of the Lancashire cotton industry. The cotton workers' vote was such a large proportion of the total that if it was mobilised it would be as decisive as that of the miners in mining areas. Their vote had sent a Radical Liberal to Parliament unopposed at the last election. What now? In the wake of the Taff Vale decisions the move for independent labour representation was growing. This posed the possibility of a three-cornered election, Liberal and LRC candidates could split the trade union vote and conceivably let in a Conservative. The LRC worked to get a decision in favour of an independent labour candidate while the Liberals tried to get agreement on a Lib/Lab candidate under their control. The Conservatives watched the manoeuvres from the wings to see if there was a chance for them.

In the event the Conference of the Trade Unions with the ILP and the SDF endorsed the candidature of a prominent trade union official David Shackleton standing as an Independent Labour Candidate. They had ditched the Liberals.

Shackleton was elected to Parliament unopposed. For him personally and for the cotton workers it was one more step in distancing themselves from the Liberal Party.

In the autumn of 1902 Keir Hardie did take a short holiday in Scotland with his wife and then on strong medical advice another short holiday on the continent.

At the LRC Conference in 1903 it was decided that each affiliated body should contribute one penny a year for each member affiliated. This would create a Parliamentary fund out of which the LRC would pay each Member of Parliament, whose candidature had been endorsed, £200 a year. It was also agreed that all candidates endorsed should undertake to be bound by the decisions of the LRC Group in Parliament. The penalty for failing to abide by the decision of the Group would be that the Member resigned his seat. In the following year, wiser councils prevailed and the penalty was replaced by giving power to the Executive to withdraw the Member's endorsement.

The LRC by these decisions, paying MPs a salary and

establishing a Parliamentary Group discipline, moved from being a loose association to be a disciplined political party. At least it had the framework; now it needed the men to make it work. In Arthur Henderson now elected treasurer and Ramsay MacDonald the secretary, it found them. These two men along with Keir Hardie were to be the architects of the breakthrough in the 1906 election.

The campaign for the unemployed was continuous throughout the country in public meetings and articles and letters in the local and national press. In December 1902 Keir Hardie once more raised the question of unemployment in the House of Commons and was ruled out of order, quite wrongly in his view. He immediately wrote a letter on the subject that appeared in *The Times* and several other London newspapers. His appeal was that Parliament should take some action to provide work and relief to reduce suffering of these men and their families. He quoted Board of Trade and Trade Union returns showing that the number of unemployed workers was not less than half a million.

The campaign at last bore fruit in February 1903 when a two-day Conference was held at the Guildhall on the subject of unemployment. It was attended by 587 delegates. Keir Hardie shared the chairmanship of various sessions with Sir Albert Rollit MP and the Lord Mayor of Sheffield. This Conference was a triumph for Keir Hardie; no one had done more year in and year out to keep the plight of the unemployed before the people and Parliament. This was the first substantial event that recognised that more could be done about unemployment than the provision of soup kitchens. Sir John Gorst proposed that local employment bureaux be set up. Keir Hardie moved, 'that the responsibility for finding work for the unemployed should be undertaken jointly by the local authorities and central Government, and that such legislation should be introduced as would empower both central and local authorities to deal adequately with the problem.' A further resolution was adopted, 'That a permanent national organisation be formed to give effect to the decisions of the Conference....'

The fact that such a widely reported Conference had been held and its proposals subsequently ignored by the Government was valuable ammunition for the LRC. Keir Hardie made good use of it in the House, in meetings all over the country and in the *Labour Leader*. He did not forget those in need on his own doorstep. Often after midnight, when he had laid down his pen for the day, he could be seen handing out Salvation Army meal tickets to the destitute in Fleet Street and on the Embankment.

The LRC was gathering strength and in July 1903 Arthur Henderson defeated Conservative and Liberal candidates at a by-election to win Barnard Castle, Durham. That the LRC could win in Wales, Lancashire, Durham and London in spite of its limited resources gave great promise for the future.

At this important time Keir Hardie, who had been pushing himself too hard for too long, was suddenly laid low with appendicitis. Major surgery was hazardous in those days and there was great concern. Keir Hardie was now a national figure respected by his opponents, loved by his many friends, and looked to as the personification of their hopes by millions of working people who lived on the edge of destitution. Messages poured in from all parts of Britain and from overseas, not only from friends but from political opponents and from King Edward himself who had recently undergone the same operation.

The operation was successful but he had to curtail his activities. In January 1904 Keir Hardie handed over the *Labour Leader* to the Independent Labour Party to be their official journal. He continued to write for it for the rest of his life, but he would be relieved of the responsibility of the editorship, management and finance. He wrote, 'The thought of parting with it is like consenting to the loss of a deeply loved child.... But I have no longer the spring or elasticity of a few years ago....'

He spent the early months of 1904 in his home in Cumnock with his books, his garden and his family. In the spring he had a real holiday in the South of France. Ramsay MacDonald travelled with him and stayed on for part of the time. He returned in June looking well but not fully restored to his old vitality. This is not to say that his vision or indeed his physical capacity was not still formidable; he was after all still two years short of his fiftieth birthday.

In September he again raised the unemployment problem in Parliament: Mr. Balfour, the Prime Minister, as usual played down the problem saying, 'there was no evidence of exceptional distress.' Events in the country gave the lie to this remark. There were demonstrations and marches in Manchester, Birmingham, Leeds, Liverpool, Glasgow, and industrial towns and ports throughout the country. This was now a national movement not just a local activity. Keir Hardie was in the forefront showing much of his old vigour and the local ILP branches took a major part. Keir Hardie, Will Crooks and George Lansbury met the very sympathetic Mr. Long, the President of the Local Government Board, who as a result called a conference of Guardians and Borough

Councillors in the Metropolitan area. Keir Hardie issued a statement signed by fourteen Members of Parliament setting out the facts of the situation and the powers already possessed by local authorities and Boards of Guardians. He proposed a new state department with a Minister of Industry, and a new set of administrative councils to start projects for roads, afforestation, and foreshore reclamation. It was a great satisfaction to Keir Hardie to have now by his side, in Parliament, Will Crooks with his unrivalled experience of this kind of work. With all this publicity as a background to the November municipal elections there was a large increase in Labour representation across the country.

In April 1905 the Government produced its 'Unemployed Workmans Bill' and conceded the principle of state responsibility for the unemployed for which Keir Hardie had fought for so long. It was an enabling Bill lacking the essential financial provision, but Keir Hardie supported it because it was a starting point.

Now with the ILP he organised a series of demonstrations throughout the country demanding that each Local Authority should use the new powers given them to the full. All the time he had in mind the next General Election.

Keir Hardie was actively engaged on all fronts, such as women's rights. The ILP drafted a Bill for him to bring before Parliament at the first opportunity, the text read:

> In all matters relating to the qualification and registration of persons entitled to vote for the election of Members of Parliament whatever words occur which imply the masculine gender, shall be held to include women for all purposes connected with and having reference to the right to be registered as voters, and to vote in such elections, any law or usage to the contrary not withstanding.

Breakthrough

In November 1905 the Conservative Government collapsed and A.J. Balfour, the Prime Minister, submitted his resignation. Sir Henry Campbell-Bannerman, the Liberal Leader, having brought together the various factions in his Party, formed a Government with Asquith at the Exchequer, Grey at the Foreign Office, Haldane at the War Office, Herbert Gladstone at the Home Office, Lloyd George President of the Board of Trade and John Burns President of the Local Government Board. A formidable team. However, it was not Campbell-Bannerman's intention to carry on the business of Government without a majority. He promptly went to the country, the dissolution being announced on 20 December with polling to be in the middle of January 1906.

This move caught the Conservatives in disarray, as it was intended to do; Herbert Gladstone was in charge of Liberal organisation and it was in good shape. This time the LRC was also ready with fifty candidates selected that was the full number they intended to field. The Liberal hierarchy were in favour of more working class representation in Parliament and they had fully digested the lessons of the 1900 election and of the three LRC by-election victories since then. They could see the LRC winning a few more seats and in a number of seats working class votes being split between Liberal and LRC candidates, letting a Conservative in with only a minority of the votes cast. They accepted that the Lib/Lab option was no longer acceptable; the working class demand was now for independent representation. Herbert Gladstone met J. Ramsay MacDonald privately and offered that in thirty-two constituencies where the LRC was fielding a candidate no Liberal would stand in single seat constituencies and only one in two-seat constituencies. This was in no sense a general agreement; it only dealt with those thirty-two seats. The Liberals had made this sort of arrangement in the past to avoid a Liberal and a Radical fighting each other and letting a Conservative in; not for one moment did they see the LRC as a threat.

The LRC offered nothing concrete in return; they would not seek to persuade their people to vote Liberal in other seats where they had no candidate.

The election was fought mainly on the deficiencies of the Conservative Government. There was a substantial backlash over the conduct of the Boer War and the exploitation of the resources and people of Southern Africa was becoming known. Disquiet was focused on the story that cheap Chinese labour was being imported to work in the Transvaal mines. 'What about Chinese Labour' was a difficult shot to parry at an election meeting.

The most important issue was 'Free Trade.' The vast expansion of grain imports from America had resulted in a reduction of corn growing areas in England and Wales from over eight million acres to under six million acres by 1900. On the other hand ever increasing amounts of manufactured goods were being exported. Should this be left to sort itself out – 'Free Trade'; or controlled by the Government – 'Protection?.' The Conservatives were for 'Protection', the Liberals for 'Free Trade.' The LRC with rather less enthusiasm than the Liberals supported 'Free Trade.'

Unemployment, trade union legislation and social questions played little part in the election campaign except where there were working class candidates and their supporters to raise them. The LRC candidates took up strongly the need for new trade union legislation to revise the Taff Vale and other judgements and so take the legal shackles off trade union activity. They carried on the unemployment campaign and raised all the social issues such as housing, old age pensions and school meals.

The Liberal Party did not present itself as a great reforming party but was content to win the election mainly by exposing the defects of the last Conservative Government. That this was enough was a sad reflection on democracy.

The Labour Representation Committee issued a manifesto:

To the Electors
This election is to decide whether or not Labour is to be fairly represented in Parliament.
The House of Commons is supposed to be the people's House, and yet the people are not there.
Landlords, employers, lawyers, brewers, and financiers are there in force. Why not Labour?
The Trade Unions ask the same liberty as capital enjoys. They are refused.
The aged poor are neglected.
The slums remain; overcrowding continues, whilst the land goes to waste.
Shopkeepers and traders are overburdened with rates and taxation, whilst the increasing land values, which should relieve the ratepayers, go to people who have not earned them.
Wars are fought to make the rich richer, and the underfed school children are still neglected.
Chinese Labour is defended because it enriches the mine owners.
The unemployed ask for work, the Government gave them a worthless Act, and now, when you are beginning to understand the causes of your poverty, the red herring of

Protection is drawn across your path.

Protection, as experience shows, is no remedy for poverty and unemployment. It serves to keep you from dealing with the land, old age, and other social problems!

You have it in your power to see that Parliament carries out your wishes. The Labour Representation Executive appeals to you in the name of a million Trade Unionists to forget all the political differences which have kept you apart in the past and vote for –

(here is inserted the name of the Labour candidate).

Fifty LRC candidates went to the poll in the 1906 Parliamentary election. Keir Hardie took part in nearly every one of these fifty campaigns, criss-crossing the country by train and speaking at several meetings a day in crowded halls and school rooms and even in the open air in that January weather. Wherever he went he brought out the crowds and lifted the campaign.

No concessions for Keir himself; he was again opposed by two Liberals in the two-seat constituency of Methyr Tydfil. The second Liberal candidate this time, Radcliffe a Welsh shipowner, was a much more powerful candidate than the unpopular Pritchard Morgan. Keir Hardie risked defeat by spending practically the whole time touring the country; he did not arrive in Methyr until two days before the poll. He was confident that his loyal supporters would run a successful campaign. Which, of course, they did.

The LRC won twenty-nine seats in Parliament out of its fifty candidates. In addition one successful miners' candidate joined the LRC immediately after the election bringing the Parliamentary Party up to thirty members.

22 Lib/Lab members were also successful.

8 Social Democratic Federation candidates all lost.

5 Independent Socialist candidates all lost.

The Conservatives lost 180 seats.

On the facing page are set out the election results for six LRC candidates contesting the same constituency in 1900 and in 1906. Their results give an indication of the change in the political situation in those six years. The LRC vote was up in every case, generally doubled; the Liberal vote up in every case; the Conservative vote down in every case.

Name	Year	LRC	Lib.	Cons.
Philip Snowden	1900	7096	-----	**11247**
(Blackburn) 2 seats		-----	-----	**9415**
	1906	**10282**	8892	**10291**
		-----	-----	8932
Ramsay MacDonald	1900	4164	**10385**	**9066**
(Leicester) 2 seats		-----	8528	-----
	1906	**14685**	**14745**	7504
Will Thorne	1900	4419	-----	**5615**
(West Ham)	1906	**10210**	-----	4973
Keir Hardie	1900	**5745**	**8598**	-----
(Merthyr Tydfil) 2 seats	-----	-----	4004	-----
	1906	**10187**	**13971**	-----
		-----	-----	7776	-----
Fred Jowett	1900	4949	-----	**4990**
(Bradford)	1906	**4957**	3580	4147
James Parker	1900	32 76	**5543**	**5931**
(Halifax) 2 seats		-----	5325	-----
	1906	**8937**	**9354**	5041

Note: Successful candidates in bold and underlined.

For the LRC it was a breakthrough; clearly if more

seats could be fought and the Labour movement kept united there was great hope for the future.

THE FIRST PARLIAMENTARY LABOUR PARTY, 1906, ON THE TERRACE OF THE HOUSE OF COMMONS.
Standing, left to right: J. Jenkins, C. W. Bowerman, J. Hodge, J. Parker, G. D. Kelley, W. Hudson, G. J. Wardle, G. N. Barnes, F. W. Jowett, G. H. Roberts, C. Duncan, T. F. Richards, S. Walsh, A. H. Gill, Phillp Snowden, T. Summerbell, J. T. Macpherson, T. Glover, J. Seddon, J. R. Clynes, James O'Grady, Will Thorne.
Sitting, left to right: W. T. Wilson, A. Wilkie, J. Ramsay MacDonald, A. Henderson, J. Keir Hardie, D. J. Shackleton, Will Crooks.

Before the opening of the new Parliament the thirty LRC members met; they decided that they would sit on the opposition benches and be called the Labour Party. They elected their own whips and Keir Hardie as leader. They decided against a joint association with the Lib/Labs but three years later the majority of the Lib/Labs including thirteen miners crossed the floor of the House of Commons and joined the Labour Party. A few followed John Burns on to the Liberal benches and the Lib/Lab group then ceased to exist.

All the strands of Keir Hardie's pioneering work came together in the Labour Party. His own experience had convinced him of the soundness of the British House of Commons as an institution, lacking only the extension of the vote to all adult men and women. He had come to accept that his favourite child, the ILP needed a partnership with the Trade Unions to achieve adequate representation for working people in Parliament. He had broken through entrenched opposition to these developing ideas, battling on sometimes with loyal support, sometimes with none. But for him it was never an end in itself. It was a means to an end. More than that it was the expression of a belief. The belief that there was an extra dimension to life transcending our everyday material world, transcending the dogma of political parties and religious institutions, a spiritual dimension that mankind could move into and experience. In that dimension lay a new world where every man, woman and child would find a place in the sun and grow to their full potential. 'Thy will be done on earth as it is in heaven.' The challenge was to live it. Legislation alone would be an empty vessel.

When I was a small boy we had on the sideboard two huge volumes, it was as much as I could do to lift either of them. One was the family Bible, the other was *The Pilgrims Progress*. I remember looking at the illustrations in them before I could read. So it was with most, probably all of the thirty men who made up the Parliamentary

Labour Party, Christian men, mostly Methodists, heirs of John Wesley.

Few people thought that this new group in Parliament was going to get anywhere in the long run. George Bernard Shaw dissociated himself from them announcing that there was no guarantee that the Labour Party would be 'anything more than a nominally independent Trade Union and radical group.' No doubt on the evidence before him this was a rational judgement; G.B.S. was good on rational judgements, poor on acts of faith. This was an act of faith. These men with all their differences and their divisions were in so many ways inadequate for the task, but no national issue would ever again be discussed in Parliament without a strong independent voice of the working people being heard. Some of these voices would be more than a match for any ranged against them. There would be a growth of understanding and respect for the common people from all parts of the House of Commons and all sections of the community. This was a bloodless revolution.

We look back on these days with the knowledge that:

In 1906 there were 30 Labour and 370 Liberal MPs.
In 1945 there were 393 Labour and 25 Liberal MPs.
In 1906 Labour candidates received 323,195 votes.
In 1945 Labour candidates received 11,992,292 votes.

During the four years 1906 to 1910 the new Government put many Acts on the Statute book in which the Labour Party took a leading part. The Trades Disputes Act, Workmen's Compensation Act, School Meals Act, Education (Medical Inspection) Act, Small Holdings Act, Old Age Pensions, Coal Mines Eight

Hours Act, Labour Exchanges Act.

The Spectator on 25 June 1910 reported to its readers:

> The Labour Party since it came into being, has, on the whole, displayed a large amount of political wisdom. It has played its cards so well that although numerically insignificant, it has been able to a considerable extent to dominate the House of Commons, and secure legislation that neither of the other two great parties would willingly have yielded.

Keir Hardie 1913

Keir Hardie's pioneering work was at an end, the roots of Labour were established. He was now a part of a team of very able men in the House of Commons who had unique knowledge of the workings of industrial and social legislation. Five of them would be Ministers in the 1924 Labour Government, MacDonald, Snowden, Clynes, Jowett, Henderson.

Bruce Glasier had summed up the work of Keir Hardie in an address in his honour at the Annual Conference of the ILP in 1900:

> I have claimed of my comrades the privilege of moving this address as one of Keir Hardie's oldest personal friends and colleagues in the Socialist movement, and also as a fellow Scotsman. It is with some emotion that I look back on the early days of my association with him, and consider how much

has happened since then to forward the Socialist cause in our country. In those early days many of us doubted the wisdom of his political policy as we have not infrequently since had occasion to differ from him, but in most instances events have shown that his wisdom was greater than any of ours. In connection with the political issues before our Party and the country, Keir Hardie has displayed a truly marvellous insight, I would almost venture to say second sight, for indeed I do not doubt that Keir Hardie is gifted with at least a touch of that miraculous and peculiarly Scottish endowment. In the House of Commons and in the country he has established a tradition of leadership that is one of the great possessions of the socialist and Labour movement in Britain. His rocklike steadfastness, his unceasing toil, his persisting and absolute faith in the policy of his party, are qualities in which he is unexcelled by any political leader of our time. He has never failed us. Many have come and gone, but he is with us today as certainly as in the day when the ILP was formed. By night and day, often weary and often wet, he has trudged from town to city in every corner of the land bearing witness to the cause of Socialism and sturdily vindicating the cause of Independent Labour Representation. He has not stood aloof from his comrades, but has constantly been in touch with the working men and women of our movement as an everyday friend and fellow worker. He has dwelt in their houses and chatted by their firesides, and has warmed many a heart by the glow of his sympathy and companionship. The wear and tear of these many years of propaganda have told somewhat on the strength of our comrade, but he has never complained of his task nor has he grown fretful with the people or their cause. His colleagues are deeply attached to him. He is always most amenable to discussion with them. They do not always agree with his views, but they have been taught by experience to doubt their own judgement not once, but twice and thrice, when it came into conflict with his. Hardly in modern times has a man arisen from the people who, unattracted by the enticements of wealth or pleasure and unbent either by praise or abuse, has remained so faithful to the class to which he belongs. His career is a promise and a sign of an intensely earnest, capable and self reliant

214

democracy. He is a man of the people and a leader of the people.

The basis of Keir Hardie's life and work was a belief in the God-given potential in every man, woman and child. His conviction inspired working men and women to have faith in themselves and in the hate-free, greed-free, world that they could build.

The 'second sight' Glasier referred to was not special to Keir Hardie, or indeed to Scotsmen, it was available to everyone who committed themselves to the task. Keir Hardie described the experience:

> From the day that I came into public life, I have been directed by an inner life and an inner Voice. That Voice is above reason, it is beyond intellect, and the only times I have been sure of myself are when I have obeyed it.

Roots of Labour

The roots of British Labour were:

The teaching of Jesus of Nazareth as preached by John Wesley.

In the care of the poor as demonstrated by Will Crooks.

In the mobilising of a whole community as achieved by Ben Tillett.

In the hope of a new society in the writings of Robert Blatchford.

In the rousing of men and women to make democracy work by Keir Hardie.

In the lives of tens of thousands of men and women who applied one man one vote democracy in the Trade Unions, the Temperance Movement, the Cooperatives, and the Free Churches.

These men and women were dedicated to bringing about a change in the structure of society matched by a change in the behaviour of men and women. It was never in their minds that these were anything but two sides of the same coin.

The nature of the coin was expressed in the story of the Good Samaritan who looked after a man he found lying injured in the road. He cared for this man when others had passed by on the other side not because he was of his family, race or religion. He did not know whether he was a good man or a bad man, he only knew that he was in need. So he met that need.

Every man is my neighbour. To him I will give my best with no thought of recognition or reward. As we do this we build a society that does the same.

This was the way Crooks, Tillett, Blatchford,
Hardie and thousands more saw
their socialist dream
being achieved.

How do we see it now?